TRAINING
JOURNAL

_____

NAME

_____

PHONE

_____

JOURNAL DATES

REVISED & UPDATED EDITION

TRAINING JOURNAL

52 WEEKS OF

- Motivation
- Training Tips
- Cycling Wisdom
- And Much More

For Every Kind of Cyclist

BY THE EDITORS OF

RODALE.

© 2012 by Rodale Inc.

Photographs © 2012 by Rodale Inc.

Printed in the United States of America
Rodale Inc. makes every effort to use acid-free ∞, recycled paper ♻.

Photo credits for interior photographs are listed on page 180.
Book design by Christopher Rhoads

ISBN 978-1-60529-273-1 paperback

Distributed to the trade by Macmillan

2 4 6 8 10 9 7 5 3 1 paperback

We inspire and enable people to improve their lives and the world around them.
rodalebooks.com

CONTENTS

INTRODUCTION

As you've no doubt discovered on your own, training isn't a foolproof affair. You can print out all kinds of schedules and charts to meter out your base miles. You can tailor your intentions to a specific goal or upcoming event. You can fill an entire shelf with books on the subject, accumulating more and more training guides with the cat-hoarding tenacity of an elderly shut-in.

But there's no one-size-fits-all guide to getting fitter and faster. Even the best-laid training plans are only one stomach flu or Snowpocalypse from being swallowed by life's complications and time constraints.

That's where keeping a journal comes in. Specifically, the journal you now hold in your hands. Whether you've sworn to increase your miles, lose weight, or participate in your first race this year, your new journal will not only serve as a road map to cycling success, but it will also tell a more personal story of growth and progress. Fill the book with your miles and routes. Fill it with roadblocks and suc-

cesses. Fill it with funny stories and solemn oaths to never again forget sun block or chain lube or chamois cream on a six-day bike tour. Fill it up, and be prepared to learn from your victories and mistakes. Your course will be your own.

Your training needs will further emerge through the process of recording your rides, routes, and adventures. All the cycling guides in the world won't know that you're faster in the cold, or that hill climbs are where you unexpectedly excel, or that you've rated Saturday's group ride with the local bike shop a solid "12 spokes out of 18 in difficulty."

But along with your triumphs, be prepared to have your journal reveal uncomfortable truths about you. Maybe your mileage falls off when it's raining. Maybe your weight-loss efforts start to flag in mid-March. Maybe you still haven't gotten around to that New Year's resolution to sign up for your first time-trial. Maybe there's just the fact that you took the time to invent a spoke-based rating system to compare the difficulty of group rides.

When I look back at my old training journals, I see more than just a blur of numbers and mileages and snarky responses to the "Feels Like" weather report. I see that I put in more miles as the year wore on, and my race placement improved ever so slightly from the effort. I see that headwinds were more likely to crush my spirit than long climbs in the small ring. I see that in February of 2009, I was attacked by an off-leash Labradoodle and wound up on the ground before I could quick-draw my canister of Halt from its holster.

There's a story on every page and in every statistic. And being able to revisit the stories, the stats, and even the minutiae (December 2010: Ran over a dead snake and found a Chinese throwing star) is almost as helpful to me as identifying my strengths and areas for improvement. I now know how far I can push myself before encountering fatigue and needing a rest day. But I also know where I found the best ice cream in Missouri and exactly how many strangers I managed to high-five during my High-Five Challenge of January 2010 (21).

So whether you bumble your way through the training process on a wing and a prayer or upload nightly stats from a PowerTap, you'll get good use from this training journal. Write down your mileage, your interval times, your hill repeats, your lactate thresholds, your crosstraining efforts, your pounds lost, your strangers high-fived, your favorite ice cream flavors, or whatever you need to record to work toward your goals this year.

Use nutrition and training tips gathered by the editors at *Bicycling* to help you on your journey, but don't forget to also use what you learn about yourself. Even if you're just out there every night trying to spin the day's stress out of your system. You'll find purpose in keeping a log of your adventures.

May you enjoy the ride and the read.

—Caitlin Giddings

HOW TO USE THIS JOURNAL

A new year means a clean slate, so forget anything that may have happened last year to keep you from riding like you wanted to. This is the year of your big comeback, and by purchasing this training journal, you've already taken the first step toward a fitter, faster you.

So congratulations are in order. Now you just have to fill in the pages.

But don't be intimidated by the supposed mathematical seriousness of keeping a training journal. There's no plugging your lactic threshold into a spreadsheet, plotting your VO2 max rate on an X/Y axis, or calculating quadratic equations. Sure, recording basic facts about routes and mileage is a great step toward training consistency, but for the most part, this journal just provides a space to log your daily and weekly rides.

Perhaps this is the year you tackle your first charity ride, drop a few extra pounds, or just find out what's at the end of your favorite trail. Whatever you're looking for, there's something in here for you. After all, there are as many reasons to ride as there are riders. Some of us stick with it just for the thrill of bombing down hills at breakneck speed. Others get more from the sense of accomplishment that comes with beating personal bests, learning new technical skills, and squeezing in a few more miles each week.

No matter how seriously or casually you're

riding, you'll find great rewards in simply jotting down your adventures in these pages. Whether you're saddling up for your first long ride, bouncing back from an injury, or training your eyes on that top step of the podium, the process of journaling can help you assess your progress and zero in on your goals.

Journaling also helps you zero in on your toughest competitor—you. Watch your progression over the course of the year. Compete against your best times, and make note of new skills. Or just take courage from your report of the cold February morning when you launched out the door for a 20-mile slog through ice and drizzle. Now is there really any excuse not to squeeze in a quick spin on a sunny day in fall?

At the end of the year, let your training journal tell the story of goals met and miles ridden—and of trials, tribulations, and triumphs of the human spirit. Hanging with the peloton during your first big group ride. The soul-crushing misery of a flat tire on a hard day with a headwind. That cool new trail you discovered after taking a wrong turn and losing your map in the rain. Put it all in there, or just doodle in the margins next to our training tips. Doesn't that sound like a book you'd love to read at the end of the year?

Most important, don't forget to enjoy the ride.

GOALS

Good intentions can carry you only so far; focus your motivation here. Whether you vow to explore a new mountain bike trail, master a tricky road descent, or ramp up the speed on your usual loop, taking steps in the direction of your goals will keep you in the saddle and bring meaning to your rides.

Like New Year's resolutions, the more specific your ambitions are, the easier it will be to stay motivated and pick up momentum. Set long-term goals and dream rides, but don't forget to include short-term achievements that can be checked off along the way.

Maybe this will be the year you shoot for Tour de France glory, or the podium at a local cyclocross race. Or perhaps the time has come for you to pin on a race number and cross a finish line for the first time.

Whatever your aspirations, jotting down your dreams and mission statements will keep you moving forward and growing as a cyclist. But don't be afraid to update your goals over the course of the year and adapt them to your new interests, accomplishments, or even injuries. Setting goals, like cycling, is anything but static.

What are you going to do to make this the best year yet?

TRAINING JOURNAL

**Fitness starts here
and your 52 weeks
START NOW!**

TiP
of the Week

SETTING GOALS

Before you set goals, know your personality type. Baby steppers need frequent benchmarks to show incremental improvement. Big dreamers need to jolt themselves into action by signing up for an event well beyond their current abilities and telling all their friends about it so that there's no backing down.

Every time I see an adult on a bicycle, I no longer despair for the future of the human race.

—H.G. WELLS

MONDAY

ROUTE:

DISTANCE: | TIME:

NOTES:

CROSSTRAINING:

TUESDAY

ROUTE:

DISTANCE: | TIME:

NOTES:

CROSSTRAINING:

WEDNESDAY

ROUTE:

DISTANCE: | TIME:

NOTES:

CROSSTRAINING:

THURSDAY

ROUTE:

DISTANCE: | TIME:

NOTES:

CROSSTRAINING:

FRIDAY

ROUTE:

DISTANCE: | TIME:

NOTES:

CROSSTRAINING:

SATURDAY

ROUTE:

DISTANCE: | TIME:

NOTES:

CROSSTRAINING:

SUNDAY

ROUTE:

DISTANCE: | TIME:

NOTES:

CROSSTRAINING:

NOTES

WEEKLY TOTAL MILEAGE:

TOTAL MILEAGE TO DATE:

TRAINING

FIGHT THE WIND

On blustery days, pick a route that heads into the wind first. Then slide into the drops and bring your elbows and knees tight to your body to minimize drag. In a group, ride in a single-file paceline to slice through headwinds. If the breeze is whipping sideways, form an angled paceline by overlapping your front wheel with the rear wheel of the rider ahead of you to keep the wind out of your face. Pedal at a higher-than-normal cadence even if it means riding a little slower. Then, turn around and enjoy a tailwind as you speed home.

of the Week

CONSISTENT MILEAGE

The key for new riders is logging consistent saddle time. You can begin building endurance and acclimating your body to the bike with rides as short as 15 to 20 minutes. Simple jaunts around the block are better than nothing.

*Ride your bike,
ride your bike,
ride your bike.*

—FAUSTO COPPI, on what it takes to become a champion

MONDAY
ROUTE:

DISTANCE: | TIME:

NOTES:

CROSSTRAINING:

TUESDAY
ROUTE:

DISTANCE: | TIME:

NOTES:

CROSSTRAINING:

WEDNESDAY
ROUTE:

DISTANCE: | TIME:

NOTES:

CROSSTRAINING:

THURSDAY
ROUTE:

DISTANCE: | TIME:

NOTES:

CROSSTRAINING:

FRIDAY
ROUTE:

DISTANCE: | TIME:

NOTES:

CROSSTRAINING:

SATURDAY

ROUTE:

DISTANCE: | TIME:

NOTES:

CROSSTRAINING:

SUNDAY

ROUTE:

DISTANCE: | TIME:

NOTES:

CROSSTRAINING:

NOTES

Nutrition

THINK BEFORE YOU DRINK

If you're looking to lose a few pounds, watch out for beverages, which can contain surprising amounts of calories. Limit sugar and creamer in coffee, and dilute juice with seltzer to make a low-calorie soda. And save the big glasses for water— caloric drinks such as milk and smoothies are best sipped from small cups so you don't end up taking in a meal's worth of calories through a straw.

WEEKLY TOTAL MILEAGE:

TOTAL MILEAGE TO DATE:

TiP
of the Week

RIDING DURING WINTER

Snow days might not be as exciting as they were when you were a kid, but with the right preparation, they can liven up your ride without putting a damper on your training or commute.

Seal Out the Cold. Never leave home without a waterproof, windproof shell over your base layers. For colder temperatures, consider wearing a balaclava and even ski goggles to protect your face.

Stay Loose. You're more likely to fishtail in the snow, but if you keep pedaling and relax, your bike will follow its natural instinct to stay upright. If you hit a sketchy patch, keep your weight centered, don't brake or try to steer out of it, and roll through it.

Avoid the Beaten Track. Fresh snow is usually the easiest type to pedal on. Be smart about choosing lines. If you do topple, your extra clothing—and the snowbanks—will help cushion your fall.

MONDAY

ROUTE:

DISTANCE: | TIME:

NOTES:

CROSSTRAINING:

TUESDAY

ROUTE:

DISTANCE: | TIME:

NOTES:

CROSSTRAINING:

WEDNESDAY

ROUTE:

DISTANCE: | TIME:

NOTES:

CROSSTRAINING:

THURSDAY

ROUTE:

DISTANCE: | TIME:

NOTES:

CROSSTRAINING:

FRIDAY

ROUTE:

DISTANCE: | TIME:

NOTES:

CROSSTRAINING:

SATURDAY

ROUTE:

DISTANCE: TIME:

NOTES:

CROSSTRAINING:

SUNDAY

ROUTE:

DISTANCE: TIME:

NOTES:

CROSSTRAINING:

NOTES

WEEKLY TOTAL MILEAGE:

TOTAL MILEAGE TO DATE:

TRAINING

POWER TUNES

Addicted to your iPod? Listening to music during exercise recovery can clear lactate more quickly and reduce perceived rate of exertion. And a recent study reports that when you choose the music, performance during an explosive exercise increases even more. Use an online BPM analyzer to calculate the beats per minute of the songs in your library, and match your playlist to your effort for maximum power.

> *The bicycle, the bicycle surely, should always be the vehicle of novelists and poets.*
>
> —CHRISTOPHER MORLEY

TiP
of the Week

COLD RIDES MELT POUNDS

Having trouble getting out the door this month? Winter rides can help you get lean by activating brown fat, which, unlike regular fat, is only triggered by cold weather and burns calories instead of storing them. Fully activated brown fat can raise your resting metabolism by 20 percent—enough to trim off 9 pounds a year.

> *There are too many factors you have to take into account that you have no control over . . . The most important factor you can keep in your own hands is yourself. I always placed the greatest emphasis on that.*

— EDDY MERCKX

MONDAY
ROUTE:

DISTANCE: | TIME:

NOTES:

CROSSTRAINING:

TUESDAY
ROUTE:

DISTANCE: | TIME:

NOTES:

CROSSTRAINING:

WEDNESDAY
ROUTE:

DISTANCE: | TIME:

NOTES:

CROSSTRAINING:

THURSDAY
ROUTE:

DISTANCE: | TIME:

NOTES:

CROSSTRAINING:

FRIDAY
ROUTE:

DISTANCE: | TIME:

NOTES:

CROSSTRAINING:

SATURDAY

ROUTE:

DISTANCE: _____ TIME: _____

NOTES: _____

CROSSTRAINING: _____

SUNDAY

ROUTE:

DISTANCE: _____ TIME: _____

NOTES: _____

CROSSTRAINING: _____

NOTES

_____
_____
_____
_____
_____
_____
_____
_____
_____
_____
_____
_____
_____
_____

WEEKLY TOTAL MILEAGE:

TOTAL MILEAGE TO DATE:

TRAINING

MAKE RIDE TIME

Having trouble finding time to ride consistently? Small changes can help you stick to your training. First, pick a time to ride and stick to it. If darkness or weather interferes, set up the trainer. And then recruit a friend—it's harder to bail on a workout if someone's counting on you to show. But also, be open to spontaneity. If you get a spare half an hour, get on your bike; that's 30 minutes you weren't riding before. Finally, make sure you have a goal you're working toward.

TiP
of the Week

FIND THE RIGHT SADDLE HEIGHT

With your cycling shoes on, sit on the saddle (have someone stand in front of you and hold the bike upright) and grab the handlebar. Let your legs hang straight down. Rotate the right crank to its lowest position. Without rocking your hips, place your right heel onto the pedal. Your heel should barely reach the pedal. If your knee is bent, raise the saddle. If your heel doesn't reach the pedal, lower the saddle until your heel makes contact. Be sure the saddle is parallel to the ground (not the top tube) and the correct distance behind the bottom bracket—your shop will have to calculate this. Record your saddle height.

MONDAY
ROUTE:

DISTANCE: | TIME:

NOTES:

CROSSTRAINING:

TUESDAY
ROUTE:

DISTANCE: | TIME:

NOTES:

CROSSTRAINING:

WEDNESDAY
ROUTE:

DISTANCE: | TIME:

NOTES:

CROSSTRAINING:

THURSDAY
ROUTE:

DISTANCE: | TIME:

NOTES:

CROSSTRAINING:

FRIDAY
ROUTE:

DISTANCE: | TIME:

NOTES:

CROSSTRAINING:

SATURDAY

ROUTE:

DISTANCE: | TIME:

NOTES:

CROSSTRAINING:

SUNDAY

ROUTE:

DISTANCE: | TIME:

NOTES:

CROSSTRAINING:

NOTES

WEEKLY TOTAL MILEAGE:

TOTAL MILEAGE TO DATE:

Maintenance

PREVENT FLAT TIRES

Want to ensure that you won't flat? Here's how:

1. Dust your tubes with talcum powder. A light coat of talcum powder will keep the tube from becoming stuck against the inside of your tire and will decrease the chance of a pinch-flat.

2. Slime 'em. Inject a puncture-resistant solution such as Slime into your tubes. It adds weight (roughly 50 to 100 grams per wheel) but makes your tires nearly flat-proof.

3. Go tubeless. Try a tubeless system. Because there's no tube, you can't pinch flat. Tubeless tires use slightly thicker rubber, meaning you're not likely to have a flat from a puncture.

The ultimate measure of a man is not where he stands in moments of comfort, but where he stands at times of challenge and controversy.

—Martin Luther King Jr.

TiP
of the Week

TAKE THE LANE

You have a right to the road, so use it. It's safer than riding on the shoulder, which is often cracked, covered in gravel, or worse. But don't be a road hog, either—share the lane.

I've read that I flew up the hills and mountains of France. But you don't fly up a hill. You struggle slowly and painfully up a hill, and maybe, if you work very hard, you get to the top ahead of everybody else.

—LANCE ARMSTRONG

MONDAY

ROUTE:

DISTANCE: | TIME:

NOTES:

CROSSTRAINING:

TUESDAY

ROUTE:

DISTANCE: | TIME:

NOTES:

CROSSTRAINING:

WEDNESDAY

ROUTE:

DISTANCE: | TIME:

NOTES:

CROSSTRAINING:

THURSDAY

ROUTE:

DISTANCE: | TIME:

NOTES:

CROSSTRAINING:

FRIDAY

ROUTE:

DISTANCE: | TIME:

NOTES:

CROSSTRAINING:

SATURDAY

ROUTE:

DISTANCE: _____ | TIME: _____

NOTES:

CROSSTRAINING:

SUNDAY

ROUTE:

DISTANCE: _____ | TIME: _____

NOTES:

CROSSTRAINING:

NOTES

_____
_____
_____
_____
_____
_____
_____
_____
_____
_____
_____
_____
_____

WEEKLY TOTAL MILEAGE:

TOTAL MILEAGE TO DATE:

Nutrition

BALANCE YOUR DIET

Picture your plate as a clock. Ten to 15 "minutes" of that plate should hold lean protein, such as grilled chicken, fish, lean beef, lean pork, soybeans, or eggs. Dedicate 20 minutes for whole grains. Vegetables and fruits fill out the remainder of the clock. Feel free to throw in healthy fats, like a handful of nuts or a tablespoon of olive or canola oil.

TiP
of the Week

CORNERING

Turn corners with confidence in these three easy steps: Enter wide, exit wide, and try to ease up on your brakes. It sounds counterintuitive, but the harder you yank on your brake levers, the less control you have over your bike. The best riders slow well before a corner. Plus, laying off the stoppers forces you to focus on key cornering skills such as weight distribution, body position, and line choice.

Only those who risk going too far can possibly find out how far one can go.

—T.S. Eliot

MONDAY

ROUTE:

DISTANCE: | TIME:

NOTES:

CROSSTRAINING:

TUESDAY

ROUTE:

DISTANCE: | TIME:

NOTES:

CROSSTRAINING:

WEDNESDAY

ROUTE:

DISTANCE: | TIME:

NOTES:

CROSSTRAINING:

THURSDAY

ROUTE:

DISTANCE: | TIME:

NOTES:

CROSSTRAINING:

FRIDAY

ROUTE:

DISTANCE: | TIME:

NOTES:

CROSSTRAINING:

SATURDAY

ROUTE:

DISTANCE: | TIME:

NOTES:

CROSSTRAINING:

SUNDAY

ROUTE:

DISTANCE: | TIME:

NOTES:

CROSSTRAINING:

NOTES

WEEKLY TOTAL MILEAGE:

TOTAL MILEAGE TO DATE:

Nutrition

WINTER POWER CARBS

Limited sunlight can lower levels of serotonin, the feel-good hormone, and make you crave comfort foods, such as starchy carbs. Beans provide those carbs, as well as satiating protein and filling fiber (a cup has 12 grams). And findings from the National Nutrition and Health Examination Survey show that people who eat beans weigh seven pounds less on average than those who snub them.

TiP
of the Week

SPICE UP YOUR DIET

Did you know that one teaspoon of cinnamon delivers as many antioxidants as a cup of pomegranate juice? Add antioxidant-rich herbs and spices such as oregano, cinnamon, or dill to entrees, and your muscles will thank you: Antioxidant-rich herbs and spices can repair the wear and tear from long rides.

I have always struggled to achieve excellence. One thing that cycling has taught me is that if you can achieve something without a struggle, it's not going to be satisfying.

— GREG LEMOND

MONDAY
ROUTE:

DISTANCE: | TIME:

NOTES:

CROSSTRAINING:

TUESDAY
ROUTE:

DISTANCE: | TIME:

NOTES:

CROSSTRAINING:

WEDNESDAY
ROUTE:

DISTANCE: | TIME:

NOTES:

CROSSTRAINING:

THURSDAY
ROUTE:

DISTANCE: | TIME:

NOTES:

CROSSTRAINING:

FRIDAY
ROUTE:

DISTANCE: | TIME:

NOTES:

CROSSTRAINING:

SATURDAY

ROUTE:

DISTANCE: | TIME:

NOTES:

CROSSTRAINING:

SUNDAY

ROUTE:

DISTANCE: | TIME:

NOTES:

CROSSTRAINING:

NOTES

WEEKLY TOTAL MILEAGE:

TOTAL MILEAGE TO DATE:

TRAINING

RIDE HARD

It's a simple formula: To get faster, you need to ride faster. Intervals squeeze every drop of fitness from your time on the bike. Try the following two or three times a week: Choose a route that includes a climb or stretch of road where you can go nearly all-out for 3 to 5 minutes. Warm up for 15 to 30 minutes, then ride hard—your exertion should be about a 7 out of 10—for 3 minutes. Recover for 90 seconds, then repeat the sequence four more times.

TiP
of the Week

TURN WITH YOUR KNEES

On a fast descent, clamp your knees tight against the top tube. That'll keep the bike from vibrating at high speed and allow you to use small weight shifts to steer instead of turning the handlebar.

Let me tell you what I think of bicycling. I think it has done more to emancipate women than anything else in the world. It gives women a feeling of freedom and self-reliance. I stand and rejoice every time I see a woman ride by on a wheel . . . the picture of free, untrammeled womanhood.

—SUSAN B. ANTHONY

MONDAY

ROUTE:

DISTANCE: | TIME:

NOTES:

CROSSTRAINING:

TUESDAY

ROUTE:

DISTANCE: | TIME:

NOTES:

CROSSTRAINING:

WEDNESDAY

ROUTE:

DISTANCE: | TIME:

NOTES:

CROSSTRAINING:

THURSDAY

ROUTE:

DISTANCE: | TIME:

NOTES:

CROSSTRAINING:

FRIDAY

ROUTE:

DISTANCE: | TIME:

NOTES:

CROSSTRAINING:

SATURDAY

ROUTE:

DISTANCE: _____ TIME: _____

NOTES: _____

CROSSTRAINING: _____

SUNDAY

ROUTE:

DISTANCE: _____ TIME: _____

NOTES: _____

CROSSTRAINING: _____

NOTES

_____
_____
_____
_____
_____
_____
_____
_____
_____
_____
_____
_____

WEEKLY TOTAL MILEAGE:

TOTAL MILEAGE TO DATE:

Nutrition

RAISING THE BAR

Need help choosing an energy bar that won't weigh you down? Go for bars with a higher percentage of calories from carbohydrates than from protein or fat, or about 10 grams of protein and 7 grams of fat for every 20 to 25 grams of carbs. But make sure the ingredient list doesn't read like a chemistry quiz; healthy fuel contains whole ingredients such as dried fruit, oats, and honey.

TiP
of the Week

SURVIVE A FRONT FLAT TIRE

Imagine that as you enter a corner, your front tire blows out. A worst-case scenario for sure, but one you can survive if you have your wits together. As soon as the flat hits, stop leaning on the bike. Once you have it upright, you can apply the rear brake—under no circumstances should you hit the front brake. Once you have the bike slowed down, clip your foot out and, with your weight as far back as possible, put your foot on the ground. You've just survived a front flat.

If you brake, you don't win.

—MARIO CIPOLLINI

MONDAY

ROUTE:

DISTANCE: | TIME:

NOTES:

CROSSTRAINING:

TUESDAY

ROUTE:

DISTANCE: | TIME:

NOTES:

CROSSTRAINING:

WEDNESDAY

ROUTE:

DISTANCE: | TIME:

NOTES:

CROSSTRAINING:

THURSDAY

ROUTE:

DISTANCE: | TIME:

NOTES:

CROSSTRAINING:

FRIDAY

ROUTE:

DISTANCE: | TIME:

NOTES:

CROSSTRAINING:

SATURDAY

ROUTE:

DISTANCE: | TIME:

NOTES:

CROSSTRAINING:

SUNDAY

ROUTE:

DISTANCE: | TIME:

NOTES:

CROSSTRAINING:

NOTES

WEEKLY TOTAL MILEAGE:

TOTAL MILEAGE TO DATE:

Nutrition

MORNING FUEL

Wondering whether to skip the oatmeal this morning? Studies show that endurance athletes burn equal amounts of fat regardless of whether they fasted or fueled pre-workout. But when you eat a little something before a ride, you get a bonus calorie burn when your body fires up its digestive system and a better workout overall.

TiP
of the Week

FIND A GOOD COACH

Cycling's governing body in America, USA Cycling, has a licensing and certification program that ensures the quality of the coaches that it sanctions. Regardless of certification level—USA Cycling has three—the best coach for you is one who fits your style and can help you develop into a more complete cyclist, by teaching skills, strategy, tactics, nutrition, etc. You can find a list of all USA Cycling–certified coaches at www .usacycling.org/coaches.

If you worried about falling off the bike, you'd never get on.

—LANCE ARMSTRONG

MONDAY

ROUTE:

DISTANCE: | TIME:

NOTES:

CROSSTRAINING:

TUESDAY

ROUTE:

DISTANCE: | TIME:

NOTES:

CROSSTRAINING:

WEDNESDAY

ROUTE:

DISTANCE: | TIME:

NOTES:

CROSSTRAINING:

THURSDAY

ROUTE:

DISTANCE: | TIME:

NOTES:

CROSSTRAINING:

FRIDAY

ROUTE:

DISTANCE: | TIME:

NOTES:

CROSSTRAINING:

SATURDAY

ROUTE:

DISTANCE: | TIME:

NOTES:

CROSSTRAINING:

SUNDAY

ROUTE:

DISTANCE: | TIME:

NOTES:

CROSSTRAINING:

NOTES

EQUIPMENT

STAY READY

You never know when you'll have the chance to sneak in a workout. Borrowing or renting a bike is easy, but it's harder to find a spare helmet, shoes, and chamois. Keep an extra kit in your car to make sure you never miss a chance for an impromptu ride. Scour bike swaps for secondhand shoes, pedals, and other items, but buy a new helmet—decent models can be found for about $75.

WEEKLY TOTAL MILEAGE:

TOTAL MILEAGE TO DATE:

TiP
of the Week

GET RID OF SADDLE SORES

Are your bike shorts starting to feel like a belt sander while you pedal? Take a few days off the bike, and keep areas affected by saddle sores clean and dry. Diaper-rash and antibiotic creams can soothe the pain and speed up healing, but to prevent sores from returning, adjust your saddle height to reduce chafing and side-to-side hip rocking, and invest in shorts with a seamless chamois, wash them between rides, and lube up with chamois cream.

Life is like riding a bicycle. To keep your balance, you must keep moving.

—ALBERT EINSTEIN

MONDAY

ROUTE:

DISTANCE: | TIME:

NOTES:

CROSSTRAINING:

TUESDAY

ROUTE:

DISTANCE: | TIME:

NOTES:

CROSSTRAINING:

WEDNESDAY

ROUTE:

DISTANCE: | TIME:

NOTES:

CROSSTRAINING:

THURSDAY

ROUTE:

DISTANCE: | TIME:

NOTES:

CROSSTRAINING:

FRIDAY

ROUTE:

DISTANCE: | TIME:

NOTES:

CROSSTRAINING:

SATURDAY

ROUTE:

DISTANCE: | TIME:

NOTES:

CROSSTRAINING:

SUNDAY

ROUTE:

DISTANCE: | TIME:

NOTES:

CROSSTRAINING:

NOTES

WEEKLY TOTAL MILEAGE:

TOTAL MILEAGE TO DATE:

Maintenance

CHECK YOUR TIRE PRESSURE

Keep rolling and prevent flats with these easy tips:

• **Road/commuter:** If you weigh more than 180 pounds, inflate to the maximum on the tire sidewall. If you weigh 110 or less, fill to the minimum. Inflate to somewhere in between accordingly.

• **Mountain bike:** Target somewhere between 27 and 32 pounds per square inch (psi) for most tires. Ultraskinny XC tires may require as much as 35 psi. Figure on 20 to 30 psi for tubeless tires.

TiP
of the Week

VARIETY AIDS RECOVERY

Got sore muscles?
After your next long ride, try eating a combination of antioxidant-and flavonoid-rich foods (such as strawberries, kale, and fish) to reduce inflammation.

Consider a man riding a bicycle. Whoever he is, we can say three things about him. We know he got on the bicycle and started to move. We know that at some point he will stop and get off. Most important of all, we know that if at any point between the beginning and the end of his journey he stops moving and does not get off the bicycle, he will fall off it. That is a metaphor for the journey through life of any living thing, and I think of any society of living things.

—WILLIAM GOLDING
author of *A Moving Target*

MONDAY
ROUTE:

DISTANCE: | TIME:

NOTES:

CROSSTRAINING:

TUESDAY
ROUTE:

DISTANCE: | TIME:

NOTES:

CROSSTRAINING:

WEDNESDAY
ROUTE:

DISTANCE: | TIME:

NOTES:

CROSSTRAINING:

THURSDAY
ROUTE:

DISTANCE: | TIME:

NOTES:

CROSSTRAINING:

FRIDAY
ROUTE:

DISTANCE: | TIME:

NOTES:

CROSSTRAINING:

SATURDAY

ROUTE:

DISTANCE: | TIME:

NOTES:

CROSSTRAINING:

SUNDAY

ROUTE:

DISTANCE: | TIME:

NOTES:

CROSSTRAINING:

NOTES

WEEKLY TOTAL MILEAGE:

TOTAL MILEAGE TO DATE:

Nutrition

GET BUZZED

New research shows caffeinated drinks aren't the dangerous, dehydrating diuretic once thought. In fact, caffeine can actually improve your workout by lowering your perceived exertion while improving your strength, endurance, and mental performance. If you're looking for a grande-size carb burn, try a caffeinated sports beverage, which speeds glucose absorption in the intestine.

TiP
of the Week

ONE MOVE FOR FULL-BODY STRENGTH

A strong core will keep your legs from fatiguing and could prevent neck and back injuries, improve performance, and even speed recovery. Do this move 3 or 4 days a week to target core cycling muscles in your shoulders, upper back, obliques, and abdominals. Hold an 8- to 10-pound dumbbell in your right hand and prop your body on your left forearm in a side plank position. Extend your right arm in front of you at shoulder level, then slowly raise the weight toward the ceiling. Lower. That's one rep. Do 10, then switch sides.

MONDAY

ROUTE:

DISTANCE: | TIME:

NOTES:

CROSSTRAINING:

TUESDAY

ROUTE:

DISTANCE: | TIME:

NOTES:

CROSSTRAINING:

WEDNESDAY

ROUTE:

DISTANCE: | TIME:

NOTES:

CROSSTRAINING:

THURSDAY

ROUTE:

DISTANCE: | TIME:

NOTES:

CROSSTRAINING:

FRIDAY

ROUTE:

DISTANCE: | TIME:

NOTES:

CROSSTRAINING:

SATURDAY

ROUTE:

DISTANCE: | TIME:

NOTES:

CROSSTRAINING:

SUNDAY

ROUTE:

DISTANCE: | TIME:

NOTES:

CROSSTRAINING:

NOTES

WEEKLY TOTAL MILEAGE:

TOTAL MILEAGE TO DATE:

Nutrition

BAR NONE

Headed out for a quick loop? The biggest food mistake recreational cyclists make is eating too much on short rides. On rides that last less than 2 hours, leave energy foods at home. You're not burning enough to warrant the extra calories.

It is by riding a bicycle that you learn the contours of a country best, since you have to sweat up the hills and coast down them. Thus you remember them as they actually are, while in a motor car only a high hill impresses you.

—ERNEST HEMINGWAY

TiP
of the Week

HYDRATE ON THE GO

Guzzling gallons of fluids before a ride will do little more than send you searching for rest stops. Instead, sip a 16-ounce sports drink an hour or two before you saddle up. That's enough time for your body to absorb what it needs and eliminate what it doesn't. Then take in about 6 to 8 ounces (two or three gulps) every 15 to 20 minutes while you ride.

Cycle tracks will abound in Utopia.

—H.G. WELLS

MONDAY

ROUTE:

DISTANCE: | TIME:

NOTES:

CROSSTRAINING:

TUESDAY

ROUTE:

DISTANCE: | TIME:

NOTES:

CROSSTRAINING:

WEDNESDAY

ROUTE:

DISTANCE: | TIME:

NOTES:

CROSSTRAINING:

THURSDAY

ROUTE:

DISTANCE: | TIME:

NOTES:

CROSSTRAINING:

FRIDAY

ROUTE:

DISTANCE: | TIME:

NOTES:

CROSSTRAINING:

SATURDAY

ROUTE:

DISTANCE: | TIME:

NOTES:

CROSSTRAINING:

SUNDAY

ROUTE:

DISTANCE: | TIME:

NOTES:

CROSSTRAINING:

NOTES

WEEKLY TOTAL MILEAGE:

TOTAL MILEAGE TO DATE:

TRAINING

BACK SUPPORT

Your lower back supports you while you ride, no matter how much you abuse it. No wonder it protests sometimes. Show your back some love—and prevent the nagging pain that's so common on long rides—by strengthening your abs, obliques, and back with core exercises two or 3 days a week. Also, make sure your bike fit is dialed in, or perfectly adjusted. Being too stretched out over the top tube puts undue strain on the muscles that support your spine.

TiP
of the Week

GROUP UP

Whether you're embarking on a 500-mile charity ride or racing Paris-Nice, there's safety in numbers. Teammates and friends can pull if you're feeling tired, share their food, or help fix a mechanical. "I've seen this so many times," says Chris Horner, 2011 Tour of California winner. "A guy is leading the race and is really strong, and so he goes into a breakaway. But what happens if he crashes or flats? He is all alone. Stay with your group as long as possible."

Machines don't break records. Muscles do.

—LON HALDEMAN,
winner of the 1982
Great American Bike Race

MONDAY

ROUTE:

DISTANCE:	TIME:

NOTES:

CROSSTRAINING:

TUESDAY

ROUTE:

DISTANCE:	TIME:

NOTES:

CROSSTRAINING:

WEDNESDAY

ROUTE:

DISTANCE:	TIME:

NOTES:

CROSSTRAINING:

THURSDAY

ROUTE:

DISTANCE:	TIME:

NOTES:

CROSSTRAINING:

FRIDAY

ROUTE:

DISTANCE:	TIME:

NOTES:

CROSSTRAINING:

SATURDAY

ROUTE:

DISTANCE: | TIME:

NOTES:

CROSSTRAINING:

SUNDAY

ROUTE:

DISTANCE: | TIME:

NOTES:

CROSSTRAINING:

NOTES

WEEKLY TOTAL MILEAGE:

TOTAL MILEAGE TO DATE:

Nutrition

CARB CONTROL

Choose carbs wisely. Eat starchy, quick-digesting carbs only during and right before and after training rides or races, when it's important to get food that can be quickly digested and converted to fuel. Otherwise, get your carbs from fruits and vegetables.

TiP
of the Week

TEAR REPAIR

Need to bandage a tire mid-ride? Fold a dollar bill in half (George's face will be creased down the middle) and then in half again (same direction). With the tube removed, place the quartered currency on the inside of the tire, against the slice. Reinstall the tube and inflate to the proper psi. No cash? Use a spent energy-bar wrapper or gel packet.

I always had and I still have that special desire in me to be the best....That's why I accept, and that's why I am proud of the nickname that they once gave me.

— EDDY "The Cannibal"
MERCKX

MONDAY

ROUTE:

DISTANCE: | TIME:

NOTES:

CROSSTRAINING:

TUESDAY

ROUTE:

DISTANCE: | TIME:

NOTES:

CROSSTRAINING:

WEDNESDAY

ROUTE:

DISTANCE: | TIME:

NOTES:

CROSSTRAINING:

THURSDAY

ROUTE:

DISTANCE: | TIME:

NOTES:

CROSSTRAINING:

FRIDAY

ROUTE:

DISTANCE: | TIME:

NOTES:

CROSSTRAINING:

SATURDAY

ROUTE:

DISTANCE: | TIME:

NOTES:

CROSSTRAINING:

SUNDAY

ROUTE:

DISTANCE: | TIME:

NOTES:

CROSSTRAINING:

NOTES

WEEKLY TOTAL MILEAGE:

TOTAL MILEAGE TO DATE:

TRAINING

GOING LONG

The key to building endurance is to pace yourself and start way slower than you want to. A quarter of the way in, evaluate how you're feeling and tweak your effort up or down accordingly. Repeat at the halfway and three-quarters marks. Only when you're 10 percent from the finish line can you really empty the tank.

TiP
of the Week

NEVER FORGET ANYTHING

The sure way to never forget anything when you're packing for a ride or a race is to have a mental checklist. Start with your helmet and work your way down—sunglasses, jacket, jersey, undershirt, shorts, socks, shoes. Then think about your bike—starting with your pump and spare tube—before ending with water bottles and energy food, perhaps. Whatever order you use, always keep it the same and you'll be unlikely to forget even the smallest detail.

I'm a big believer of the theory that you make your destiny. You've got your fate in your hands, and it's up to you, it's your responsibility. It is sometimes a heavy burden, but it's you who changes, who moves, who shapes your reality for yourself, who shapes your life.

—JENS VOIGT

MONDAY

ROUTE:

DISTANCE: | TIME:

NOTES:

CROSSTRAINING:

TUESDAY

ROUTE:

DISTANCE: | TIME:

NOTES:

CROSSTRAINING:

WEDNESDAY

ROUTE:

DISTANCE: | TIME:

NOTES:

CROSSTRAINING:

THURSDAY

ROUTE:

DISTANCE: | TIME:

NOTES:

CROSSTRAINING:

FRIDAY

ROUTE:

DISTANCE: | TIME:

NOTES:

CROSSTRAINING:

SATURDAY

ROUTE:

DISTANCE: | TIME:

NOTES:

CROSSTRAINING:

SUNDAY

ROUTE:

DISTANCE: | TIME:

NOTES:

CROSSTRAINING:

NOTES

WEEKLY TOTAL MILEAGE:

TOTAL MILEAGE TO DATE:

Nutrition

REFUEL RIGHT

The key recovery window is the 30 minutes following a ride; that's when your body needs protein to repair muscles and help reload its energy stores. Try this protein-rich smoothie: Before heading out, put 1½ scoops whey protein powder, ½ cup frozen strawberries or blueberries, ½ frozen banana, 2 tablespoons nonfat Greek yogurt, 2 tablespoons flaxseed meal, and 1 cup vanilla almond milk into a blender (but don't blend it yet). Store in the refrigerator. Whirl and drink when you return.

TiP
of the Week

TACKLE TINGLY HANDS

Hands feeling numb or weak after a long ride? You may be suffering from cyclist's palsy caused by compression of the nerve running through your wrist. The solution is taking the pressure off that nerve through proper bike fit and hand positioning. Sitting too far forward or reaching too far to the bar can place undue pressure on your palms. To avoid overextending your wrists, move your hand position often while maintaining neutral or straight wrists. If you're prone to pins and needles, stretch and strengthen your lower arms to increase your tolerance for long hours on the bar.

MONDAY

ROUTE:

DISTANCE: | TIME:

NOTES:

CROSSTRAINING:

TUESDAY

ROUTE:

DISTANCE: | TIME:

NOTES:

CROSSTRAINING:

WEDNESDAY

ROUTE:

DISTANCE: | TIME:

NOTES:

CROSSTRAINING:

THURSDAY

ROUTE:

DISTANCE: | TIME:

NOTES:

CROSSTRAINING:

FRIDAY

ROUTE:

DISTANCE: | TIME:

NOTES:

CROSSTRAINING:

SATURDAY

ROUTE:

DISTANCE: | TIME:

NOTES:

CROSSTRAINING:

SUNDAY

ROUTE:

DISTANCE: | TIME:

NOTES:

CROSSTRAINING:

NOTES

WEEKLY TOTAL MILEAGE:

TOTAL MILEAGE TO DATE:

EQUIPMENT

COMPRESSED RECOVERY

When you want to get fresh legs fast, nothing works better to speed recovery than compression socks. Studies show the socks reduce blood-lactate levels and ease muscle soreness in the calves of athletes who have worn them. For optimum effect, you may need to ignore the knee-high dork factor and wear them during hard efforts, not just afterward.

If you do what you have always done, you will get what you have always got.

—MARK TWAIN

TiP
of the Week

PIN IT

You have plenty of things to worry about on event day, but an unruly race number shouldn't be one of them. These tips will keep you flap free.

1. If you attach your number before you kit up, stretch your jersey across your lap to mimic the shape of your body. A pillow works, too, if used at home—in public, the dork factor is high.

2. Ignore any pre-punched holes in the corners. Instead, make two holes with each pin: one to go down through the number and jersey and another to come back up and out.

3. The cool kids crumple their race numbers to keep them from parachuting—but technically, that could get you disqualified. Remember: You can use more than four pins.

MONDAY
ROUTE:

DISTANCE: | TIME:

NOTES:

CROSSTRAINING:

TUESDAY
ROUTE:

DISTANCE: | TIME:

NOTES:

CROSSTRAINING:

WEDNESDAY
ROUTE:

DISTANCE: | TIME:

NOTES:

CROSSTRAINING:

THURSDAY
ROUTE:

DISTANCE: | TIME:

NOTES:

CROSSTRAINING:

FRIDAY
ROUTE:

DISTANCE: | TIME:

NOTES:

CROSSTRAINING:

SATURDAY

ROUTE:

DISTANCE: TIME:

NOTES:

CROSSTRAINING:

SUNDAY

ROUTE:

DISTANCE: TIME:

NOTES:

CROSSTRAINING:

NOTES

_____
_____
_____
_____
_____
_____
_____
_____
_____
_____
_____
_____
_____
_____

WEEKLY TOTAL MILEAGE:

TOTAL MILEAGE TO DATE:

TiP
of the Week

TAPE YOUR BARS

If you've never rewrapped your tape, now is the time to learn. Cut two 4-inch pieces of electrical tape and hang them from the top tube of your bike. Fold your brake hoods away from the bar and peel the old tape off your bars. Grab a roll of fresh tape and wrap from the bottom, making sure to keep constant pressure on the tape. At the junction of the brake lever, make a figure eight around the lever and continue wrapping. Two inches from the edge of the stem, cut the bar tape and finish it off with one of the pieces of electrical tape that you stuck on your top tube. Repeat on the remaining side of the bars.

MONDAY

ROUTE:

DISTANCE: | TIME:

NOTES:

CROSSTRAINING:

TUESDAY

ROUTE:

DISTANCE: | TIME:

NOTES:

CROSSTRAINING:

WEDNESDAY

ROUTE:

DISTANCE: | TIME:

NOTES:

CROSSTRAINING:

THURSDAY

ROUTE:

DISTANCE: | TIME:

NOTES:

CROSSTRAINING:

FRIDAY

ROUTE:

DISTANCE: | TIME:

NOTES:

CROSSTRAINING:

SATURDAY

ROUTE:

DISTANCE: | TIME:

NOTES:

CROSSTRAINING:

SUNDAY

ROUTE:

DISTANCE: | TIME:

NOTES:

CROSSTRAINING:

NOTES

TRAINING

CORE MOVES

Core strength is crucial for cycling, but crunches don't work. Try this move instead: Lie back on a mat and lift your legs so your thighs are perpendicular to the floor and your knees are bent 90 degrees. Extend your arms straight toward the ceiling. Contract your abs and lift your torso off the floor while simultaneously straightening your legs so your body forms a V. Hold for two seconds. Lower. Do three sets of 8 to 10 reps.

Most of cycling is not the Tour de France. It's not glamorous. And a lot of it is just plain hard, ugly, and miserable.

—GREG LEMOND

WEEKLY TOTAL MILEAGE:

TOTAL MILEAGE TO DATE:

TiP
of the Week

ALWAYS KEEP YOUR BIKE CLEAN

After every ride, spend 5 minutes doing the following, and you'll rarely need to wash your bike.

1. Wipe down the frame, checking for dents or cracks as you go.

2. Lube the chain with a light lubricant.

3. Inspect the sidewall of each tire for cuts or tears.

4. Spin the wheels, making sure they are true.

5. Inspect the brake pads, making sure there is no less than 2mm of usable pad. Any less, and you've got to replace them.

Pain is temporary. It may last a minute, or an hour, or a day, or a year, but eventually it will subside, and something else will take its place. If I quit, however, it lasts forever.

—LANCE ARMSTRONG

MONDAY

ROUTE:

DISTANCE: | TIME:

NOTES:

CROSSTRAINING:

TUESDAY

ROUTE:

DISTANCE: | TIME:

NOTES:

CROSSTRAINING:

WEDNESDAY

ROUTE:

DISTANCE: | TIME:

NOTES:

CROSSTRAINING:

THURSDAY

ROUTE:

DISTANCE: | TIME:

NOTES:

CROSSTRAINING:

FRIDAY

ROUTE:

DISTANCE: | TIME:

NOTES:

CROSSTRAINING:

SATURDAY

ROUTE:

DISTANCE: | TIME:

NOTES:

CROSSTRAINING:

SUNDAY

ROUTE:

DISTANCE: | TIME:

NOTES:

CROSSTRAINING:

NOTES

WEEKLY TOTAL MILEAGE:

TOTAL MILEAGE TO DATE:

Nutrition

IN A NUTSHELL

Nuts are an ideal snack for hungry cyclists. But if your go-to is peanuts or almonds, consider adding walnuts to the mix. Thanks to heart-healthy omega-3 fatty acids, people who eat a diet rich in walnuts or walnut oil have reduced blood pressure during stress—key to enjoying rides for years to come.

TiP
of the Week

CHEAT THE WIND

- Snug your clothing, and if you're racing, plaster down your number.
- Keep your bottle on the seat tube rather than the down tube.
- Shoe covers save seconds.
- Shave your legs to pare seconds off your time trials.
- The greatest drag on your bike is your body. To mitigate this, move your hands from the hoods to the drops.
- An aero helmet makes a bigger difference in slicing through the wind than aero wheels.

I didn't have the legs today, so I'll try another day.

—CADEL EVANS

MONDAY

ROUTE:

DISTANCE: | TIME:

NOTES:

CROSSTRAINING:

TUESDAY

ROUTE:

DISTANCE: | TIME:

NOTES:

CROSSTRAINING:

WEDNESDAY

ROUTE:

DISTANCE: | TIME:

NOTES:

CROSSTRAINING:

THURSDAY

ROUTE:

DISTANCE: | TIME:

NOTES:

CROSSTRAINING:

FRIDAY

ROUTE:

DISTANCE: | TIME:

NOTES:

CROSSTRAINING:

SATURDAY

ROUTE:

DISTANCE: | TIME:

NOTES:

CROSSTRAINING:

SUNDAY

ROUTE:

DISTANCE: | TIME:

NOTES:

CROSSTRAINING:

NOTES

WEEKLY TOTAL MILEAGE:

TOTAL MILEAGE TO DATE:

Nutrition

LOSE 5 POUNDS IN 5 WEEKS

Cut 500 calories per day from your diet, and you'll drop a pound a week. Start by targeting sweet foods and alcohol; they stimulate the overproduction of insulin, which makes you crave even more food and promotes the storage of fat, even if you're on a low-calorie diet.

TiP
of the Week

DESCEND WITH EASE

Descending takes finesse and confidence, which come with practice. Start with a short, straight downhill and practice getting into the correct position. Shift your rear back, spread out your weight, and put your hands in the drops to lower your center of gravity. Scrub speed by gently squeezing the brakes, going easy on the front brake. And be cautious in turns: Slow down gradually so you're at a comfortable speed when you reach a turn and lean your bike, not your body. Then look where you want to go, and flatten the turn by starting wide, cutting through the apex, and exiting wide.

Don't buy upgrades; ride up grades.

—EDDY MERCKX

MONDAY

ROUTE:

DISTANCE: | TIME:

NOTES:

CROSSTRAINING:

TUESDAY

ROUTE:

DISTANCE: | TIME:

NOTES:

CROSSTRAINING:

WEDNESDAY

ROUTE:

DISTANCE: | TIME:

NOTES:

CROSSTRAINING:

THURSDAY

ROUTE:

DISTANCE: | TIME:

NOTES:

CROSSTRAINING:

FRIDAY

ROUTE:

DISTANCE: | TIME:

NOTES:

CROSSTRAINING:

SATURDAY

ROUTE:

DISTANCE: TIME:

NOTES:

CROSSTRAINING:

SUNDAY

ROUTE:

DISTANCE: TIME:

NOTES:

CROSSTRAINING:

NOTES

WEEKLY TOTAL MILEAGE:

TOTAL MILEAGE TO DATE:

TRAINING

JUST COOL IT

Summer might seem like the best time to increase your training, but the heat can have its drawbacks. Here are three ways to stay chill when the long days and sunshine start to work against you.

• **Deflect the sun:** Pale colors reflect light, while dark ones absorb it. Try a light-colored skinsuit or a kit made with cold-black, a special fabric treatment designed to reflect sunlight.

• **Ice your legs:** Cyclists who soak their lower bodies in cold water for 20 minutes before a 40-minute time trial on a hot day generate, on average, 20 more watts of power than when they skip the soak.

• **Drink protein with carbs:** Protein helps the body retain water, so a carb-protein combo will help you go faster in 90-degree heat than only carbs would.

TiP *of the Week*

LUBE YOUR CHAIN

Clean and lube your chain with this easy pro method: Soak the center of a sponge with dish soap. With one hand, wrap the sponge around the chain, under the chainstay; then with the other hand, backpedal 10 revolutions. Rinse the sponge, squeeze out excess water, reload with dish soap, and repeat. Continue until the sponge no longer gets dirty. Dry the chain by letting it sit for 10 minutes or by backpedaling through a clean rag. Apply one drop of lube to each of the chain's pins, then backpedal 10 revolutions, allow 5 minutes for the lube to penetrate, and then wipe the chain with a clean rag by backpedaling.

MONDAY

ROUTE:

DISTANCE: | TIME:

NOTES:

CROSSTRAINING:

TUESDAY

ROUTE:

DISTANCE: | TIME:

NOTES:

CROSSTRAINING:

WEDNESDAY

ROUTE:

DISTANCE: | TIME:

NOTES:

CROSSTRAINING:

THURSDAY

ROUTE:

DISTANCE: | TIME:

NOTES:

CROSSTRAINING:

FRIDAY

ROUTE:

DISTANCE: | TIME:

NOTES:

CROSSTRAINING:

SATURDAY

ROUTE:

DISTANCE: _____ TIME: _____

NOTES:

CROSSTRAINING:

SUNDAY

ROUTE:

DISTANCE: _____ TIME: _____

NOTES:

CROSSTRAINING:

NOTES

_____
_____
_____
_____
_____
_____
_____
_____
_____
_____
_____
_____
_____

WEEKLY TOTAL MILEAGE:

TOTAL MILEAGE TO DATE:

TRAINING

RACE OUT OF A RUT

Hitting a plateau in your training? Try registering for a local race. Competition raises your fitness ceiling because it forces you to push your body harder than you do while training. You'll recover stronger and experience a bump in performance that could take weeks to develop otherwise.

If you don't accept victory graciously, you may not be able to do the same in defeat.

—MIGUEL INDURAIN, five-time Tour de France winner

TiP
of the Week

DON'T GET BURNED

The most dangerous menace on your ride may not be the squirrelly guy in front of you—it's the sun gently warming your face. Apply at least 1 ounce, or an espresso-shot worth, of sunscreen 30 minutes before your ride so your skin has time to absorb it. Make sure it gets under the edges of your clothing, which can shift as you ride and expose the skin underneath—or apply it before you kit up. Reapply every 2 hours; sooner if you're sweating profusely.

Until you put yourself to the test, there's always fear. My test is whether I can still leave the others behind on a climb like I used to before.

—MARCO PANTANI,
Tour de France and
Tour of Italy winner

MONDAY
ROUTE:

DISTANCE: | TIME:

NOTES:

CROSSTRAINING:

TUESDAY
ROUTE:

DISTANCE: | TIME:

NOTES:

CROSSTRAINING:

WEDNESDAY
ROUTE:

DISTANCE: | TIME:

NOTES:

CROSSTRAINING:

THURSDAY
ROUTE:

DISTANCE: | TIME:

NOTES:

CROSSTRAINING:

FRIDAY
ROUTE:

DISTANCE: | TIME:

NOTES:

CROSSTRAINING:

SATURDAY

ROUTE:

DISTANCE: _____ TIME: _____

NOTES:

CROSSTRAINING:

SUNDAY

ROUTE:

DISTANCE: _____ TIME: _____

NOTES:

CROSSTRAINING:

NOTES

_____
_____
_____
_____
_____
_____
_____
_____
_____
_____
_____
_____
_____
_____
_____

WEEKLY TOTAL MILEAGE:

TOTAL MILEAGE TO DATE:

EQUIPMENT

BLING YOUR BIKE

Give your frame a gold-tooth shine using a wax-free furniture polish like Pledge or a bike-specific product like Pedro's Bike Lust. First, remove dirt, grease, and debris with soapy water or a spray cleanser. Then apply polish to the frame and fork. Shine up smaller parts by spraying some on a rag. (Steer clear of your rims and brake pads.) Finish by buffing with a rag.

TiP
of the Week

COMEBACK KID

Has a traumatic crash kept you from getting back on your bike? You might recover faster if you set a goal—maybe a century or organized ride—that's several months away and then start a slow buildup to the big day.

Try not. Do. Or do not. There is no try.

—YODA

MONDAY
ROUTE:

DISTANCE: | TIME:

NOTES:

CROSSTRAINING:

TUESDAY
ROUTE:

DISTANCE: | TIME:

NOTES:

CROSSTRAINING:

WEDNESDAY
ROUTE:

DISTANCE: | TIME:

NOTES:

CROSSTRAINING:

THURSDAY
ROUTE:

DISTANCE: | TIME:

NOTES:

CROSSTRAINING:

FRIDAY
ROUTE:

DISTANCE: | TIME:

NOTES:

CROSSTRAINING:

SATURDAY

ROUTE:

DISTANCE: TIME:

NOTES:

CROSSTRAINING:

SUNDAY

ROUTE:

DISTANCE: TIME:

NOTES:

CROSSTRAINING:

NOTES

WEEKLY TOTAL MILEAGE:

TOTAL MILEAGE TO DATE:

TRAINING

SCHOOL YOUR KID

Teach your tot to bike, and you'll have a riding partner for life. This easy technique takes just three steps and doesn't involve pulling a muscle in your back.

1. Remove the pedals and lower the seat enough so your child's foot can rest flat on the ground.

2. Help her push off and have her glide to practice balance. Find a flat, paved road or path where she can build momentum yet safely stop.

3. Once she's confident, install the pedals. Help her orient the bike so one pedal is up, and tell her to push down on that pedal to get rolling.

TiP
of the Week

QUIET A CREAKY BIKE

You hear clicking and creaking from your bike, but all your necessary bolts and parts are snug. What else could it be? Assuming your quick-release skewers are tight, the sound is probably coming from one of two places: your bottom bracket or your pedals. Remove your pedals and slip pedal washers onto the spindles, then reinstall and ride. If the noise continues, check that your bottom bracket cups are tight. If you have a press-fit-type bottom bracket, take your bike to the shop.

MONDAY

ROUTE:

DISTANCE: | TIME:

NOTES:

CROSSTRAINING:

TUESDAY

ROUTE:

DISTANCE: | TIME:

NOTES:

CROSSTRAINING:

WEDNESDAY

ROUTE:

DISTANCE: | TIME:

NOTES:

CROSSTRAINING:

THURSDAY

ROUTE:

DISTANCE: | TIME:

NOTES:

CROSSTRAINING:

FRIDAY

ROUTE:

DISTANCE: | TIME:

NOTES:

CROSSTRAINING:

SATURDAY

ROUTE:

DISTANCE: | TIME:

NOTES:

CROSSTRAINING:

SUNDAY

ROUTE:

DISTANCE: | TIME:

NOTES:

CROSSTRAINING:

NOTES

WEEKLY TOTAL MILEAGE:

TOTAL MILEAGE TO DATE:

Nutrition

ORDER SURF, NOT TURF

Wanna stay lean and fast? Fatty fish, such as salmon and sardines, is rich in two essential waist whittlers: omega-3 fatty acids and vitamin D (the sunshine vitamin, which we get less of during short winter days). Both help control insulin levels and improve your ability to burn fat. One study reported that exercisers who took fish oil supplements lost more fat and gained more muscle than those who went fish oil free.

Eat before you are hungry. Drink before you are thirsty. Rest before you are tired. Cover up before you are cold. Peel off before you are hot. Don't drink or smoke on tour. Never ride just to prove yourself.

—PAUL DE Vivie, early advocate of the derailleur and 19th-century cycling journalist

TiP
of the Week

MOBILIZE ON TWO WHEELS

Cyclists have made great strides since the 1960s, but we still have work to do. Studies show that bike-friendly streets get more people riding and improve safety for everyone. It's up to us to make it happen. Find an advocacy group at peoplepoweredmovement.org. Sign up online for Clif Bar's 2-Mile Challenge to raise funds for cycling nonprofits with every mile you pedal. And while you're at it, join the League of American Bicyclists, the Adventure Cycling Association, or your local bike advocacy group.

> *Everybody wants to know what I'm on. What am I on? I'm on my bike busting my ass 6 hours a day. What are you on?*
>
> —LANCE ARMSTRONG

MONDAY

ROUTE:

DISTANCE: TIME:

NOTES:

CROSSTRAINING:

TUESDAY

ROUTE:

DISTANCE: TIME:

NOTES:

CROSSTRAINING:

WEDNESDAY

ROUTE:

DISTANCE: TIME:

NOTES:

CROSSTRAINING:

THURSDAY

ROUTE:

DISTANCE: TIME:

NOTES:

CROSSTRAINING:

FRIDAY

ROUTE:

DISTANCE: TIME:

NOTES:

CROSSTRAINING:

SATURDAY

ROUTE:

DISTANCE: | TIME:

NOTES:

CROSSTRAINING:

SUNDAY

ROUTE:

DISTANCE: | TIME:

NOTES:

CROSSTRAINING:

NOTES

Nutrition

USE YOUR NOODLE

It's okay to pass on the pasta when you're riding casually. But feel free to dish it out before a long event or training ride, especially if you're going for speed. Endurance athletes who consume more than 7 grams of carbs per kilogram of body weight (that's about 475g for a 150-pound athlete) the day before a race post faster times and maintain speed better than those who eat fewer carbs.

WEEKLY TOTAL MILEAGE:

TOTAL MILEAGE TO DATE:

TiP
of the Week

WEIGHTY ADVICE

If you're looking to add a lifting routine to your training, the order in which you hit the weights matters. Exercises considered of primary importance to meet training goals should be done first. For best cycling results, perform pedaling-muscle exercises such as leg presses, leg curls, and leg extensions before moving on.

Nothing compares to the simple pleasure of a bike ride.

—JOHN F. KENNEDY

MONDAY

ROUTE:

DISTANCE: | TIME:

NOTES:

CROSSTRAINING:

TUESDAY

ROUTE:

DISTANCE: | TIME:

NOTES:

CROSSTRAINING:

WEDNESDAY

ROUTE:

DISTANCE: | TIME:

NOTES:

CROSSTRAINING:

THURSDAY

ROUTE:

DISTANCE: | TIME:

NOTES:

CROSSTRAINING:

FRIDAY

ROUTE:

DISTANCE: | TIME:

NOTES:

CROSSTRAINING:

SATURDAY

ROUTE:

DISTANCE: | TIME:

NOTES:

CROSSTRAINING:

SUNDAY

ROUTE:

DISTANCE: | TIME:

NOTES:

CROSSTRAINING:

NOTES

WEEKLY TOTAL MILEAGE:

TOTAL MILEAGE TO DATE:

Nutrition

CHOCOLATE MILK RECOVERY

Done right, chocolate milk can be your best friend immediately after a ride. The low-fat version packs plenty of protein to repair muscles and nearly twice as many carbs as white milk to replenish glycogen stores. Sip 12 ounces within 20 minutes of finishing your ride, when muscles are most ready to absorb missing nutrients.

TiP
of the Week

FLY WITH YOUR BIKE

Does your bike love to travel as much as you do? Taking to the friendly skies with two wheels can mean baggage restrictions, careless handling, and, depending on the airline, fees as high as $175 one way. You can avoid the bike fee by bringing a bike that can be taken apart and fit into a standard-looking suitcase, as long as the packed case weighs less than 50 pounds, and you don't specifically report the contents as a "bicycle."

The bicycle is the most civilized conveyance known to man. Other forms of transport grow daily more nightmarish. Only the bicycle remains pure in heart.

—Iris Murdoch, author of *The Red and the Green*

MONDAY

ROUTE:

DISTANCE: | TIME:

NOTES:

CROSSTRAINING:

TUESDAY

ROUTE:

DISTANCE: | TIME:

NOTES:

CROSSTRAINING:

WEDNESDAY

ROUTE:

DISTANCE: | TIME:

NOTES:

CROSSTRAINING:

THURSDAY

ROUTE:

DISTANCE: | TIME:

NOTES:

CROSSTRAINING:

FRIDAY

ROUTE:

DISTANCE: | TIME:

NOTES:

CROSSTRAINING:

SATURDAY

ROUTE:

DISTANCE: | TIME:

NOTES:

CROSSTRAINING:

SUNDAY

ROUTE:

DISTANCE: | TIME:

NOTES:

CROSSTRAINING:

NOTES

_____
_____
_____
_____
_____
_____
_____
_____
_____
_____
_____
_____
_____
_____

WEEKLY TOTAL MILEAGE:

TOTAL MILEAGE TO DATE:

TRAINING

CHECK YOUR NECK

Neck and shoulders cramping up on a ride? Sit up and ride with your hands on the top of the handlebar. Move your right hand off the bar and down to your side, palm down. Straighten your arm. Drop your right shoulder slightly as you push your palm toward the pavement; lean your head to the left. You'll feel a stretch in your right neck and shoulder. Hold for a few seconds, relax, switch sides, and repeat as necessary.

TiP
of the Week

SMART SWAPS

**Instead of This >
Go for This**

- Cream cheese >
  Guacamole
- Pasta > Sweet potato
- Salmon salad on bread
  > Salmon salad in a
  romaine lettuce wrap
- Mayo > Pesto
- Doughnut > Dark
  chocolate
- Chips and pretzels >
  Mixed nuts and dried fruit
- Risotto > Mixed
  sautéed vegetables

*I never raced to
break records. I raced
to enjoy myself.*

—BERNARD HINAULT,
five-time Tour de
France winner

MONDAY

ROUTE:

DISTANCE: | TIME:

NOTES:

CROSSTRAINING:

TUESDAY

ROUTE:

DISTANCE: | TIME:

NOTES:

CROSSTRAINING:

WEDNESDAY

ROUTE:

DISTANCE: | TIME:

NOTES:

CROSSTRAINING:

THURSDAY

ROUTE:

DISTANCE: | TIME:

NOTES:

CROSSTRAINING:

FRIDAY

ROUTE:

DISTANCE: | TIME:

NOTES:

CROSSTRAINING:

SATURDAY

ROUTE:

DISTANCE: | TIME:

NOTES:

CROSSTRAINING:

SUNDAY

ROUTE:

DISTANCE: | TIME:

NOTES:

CROSSTRAINING:

NOTES

WEEKLY TOTAL MILEAGE:

TOTAL MILEAGE TO DATE:

TRAINING

CLIMB STRONGER

Want to play King of the Hill? Try "hill charges" to increase your climbing stamina. On a moderate incline, stand out of the saddle and charge up the hill as fast as possible for 30 seconds. Coast back to your starting point. Repeat, this time seated. Alternate between standing and sitting for six climbs. Recover 10 minutes, and then do another set.

TiP
of the Week

RIDING BUY WAYS

The best time to get a great deal on a new bike is the end of summer (August and September). You can expect to save between 10 and 30 percent on models that have been sitting on the floor for a few months. Although you won't have the absolute latest gear, you're likely to get a great bike at a super price, and the dealer is likely to give you an even better deal on shorts and summer clothing.

MONDAY

ROUTE:

DISTANCE: | TIME:

NOTES:

CROSSTRAINING:

TUESDAY

ROUTE:

DISTANCE: | TIME:

NOTES:

CROSSTRAINING:

WEDNESDAY

ROUTE:

DISTANCE: | TIME:

NOTES:

CROSSTRAINING:

THURSDAY

ROUTE:

DISTANCE: | TIME:

NOTES:

CROSSTRAINING:

FRIDAY

ROUTE:

DISTANCE: | TIME:

NOTES:

CROSSTRAINING:

SATURDAY

ROUTE:

DISTANCE: | TIME:

NOTES:

CROSSTRAINING:

SUNDAY

ROUTE:

DISTANCE: | TIME:

NOTES:

CROSSTRAINING:

NOTES

WEEKLY TOTAL MILEAGE:

TOTAL MILEAGE TO DATE:

TRAINING

ONE MOVE TO BEAT FATIGUE

When you get tired, your ankle joints are the first to wear out, making it hard to maintain an efficient pedal stroke. To keep riding strong, try a bent-knee heel raise two or three times a week. Stand with your feet parallel and shoulder-width apart, knees slightly bent. Raise your heels off the floor as high as you can. Pause, then slowly lower them back down. That's one rep; do three sets of 15 to 20. As they get easier, try them single-legged.

"

I need to go out and have a good time every couple weeks, go to the movies, and play golf once a week or something. I do that because I know it's going to add to my cycling.

—GREG LEMOND

"

TiP
of the Week

BINGE CONTROL

Bingeing after long rides? If you overeat after a long ride, you sabotage your recovery by making lousy choices for that all-important refueling window. The key is to make a plan: Designate one day a week as a cooking day, and spend a few hours making meals for the week and prepackaging them. That way, if you roll home hungry, there's something right-sized and healthy already waiting.

It is easy to be a holy man on a mountain bike.

—MARK W. WATSON

MONDAY

ROUTE:

DISTANCE: | TIME:

NOTES:

CROSSTRAINING:

TUESDAY

ROUTE:

DISTANCE: | TIME:

NOTES:

CROSSTRAINING:

WEDNESDAY

ROUTE:

DISTANCE: | TIME:

NOTES:

CROSSTRAINING:

THURSDAY

ROUTE:

DISTANCE: | TIME:

NOTES:

CROSSTRAINING:

FRIDAY

ROUTE:

DISTANCE: | TIME:

NOTES:

CROSSTRAINING:

SATURDAY

ROUTE:

DISTANCE: TIME:

NOTES:

CROSSTRAINING:

SUNDAY

ROUTE:

DISTANCE: TIME:

NOTES:

CROSSTRAINING:

NOTES

_____

_____

_____

_____

_____

_____

_____

_____

_____

_____

_____

_____

_____

WEEKLY TOTAL MILEAGE:

TOTAL MILEAGE TO DATE:

TRAINING

FIGHT THE PLATEAU

If your training is in a rut, you're probably doing too much of the same thing. Two possible solutions: more hours on the bike, or different riding in the time you have. If you can ride only 8 hours a week, add intensity workouts, like sprint intervals. If you often ride long and hard, take a few rest days and then add some anaerobic intervals, which involve brief, high-intensity efforts to train your fast-twitch muscles for competition. Either way, track your workouts in monthly cycles that gradually increase in intensity for 3 weeks, followed by a rest week. Then start a new cycle, only with slightly higher intensity levels.

TiP
of the Week

POST-CRASH CHECKLIST

• **Helmet:** Even if there is no visible damage to the shell, one hit and the foam layer in your helmet is toast. Check with the manufacturer to see if it has a replacement policy.

• **Frame:** Clean it, and then check for cracks, dents, and bulges. Even a scratch in the paint could eventually result in rust or corrosion.

• **Wheels and brakes:** Spin both wheels to make sure they are true and round. Feel for play in the hubs. Check spokes to be sure that none have de-tensioned. Squeeze both brake levers to ensure that the pads are centered on and still contacting the rim.

• **Steering area:** Check that you didn't bend your handlebar. Then squeeze the front brake and rock the bike to feel for play in the headset.

• **Components: Rear derailleur and cranks:** If they're bent, do not ride. **Saddle, seatpost, and pedals:** If they're damaged, replace them.

MONDAY
ROUTE:

DISTANCE: | TIME:

NOTES:

CROSSTRAINING:

TUESDAY
ROUTE:

DISTANCE: | TIME:

NOTES:

CROSSTRAINING:

WEDNESDAY
ROUTE:

DISTANCE: | TIME:

NOTES:

CROSSTRAINING:

THURSDAY
ROUTE:

DISTANCE: | TIME:

NOTES:

CROSSTRAINING:

FRIDAY
ROUTE:

DISTANCE: | TIME:

NOTES:

CROSSTRAINING:

SATURDAY

ROUTE:

DISTANCE: | TIME:

NOTES:

CROSSTRAINING:

SUNDAY

ROUTE:

DISTANCE: | TIME:

NOTES:

CROSSTRAINING:

NOTES

WEEKLY TOTAL MILEAGE:

TOTAL MILEAGE TO DATE:

Nutrition

MAGIC BEETS

A new study shows that cyclists who drink 2 cups of beetroot juice 2 hours before a time trial improve their 10-mile time by 45 seconds. The reason: Beets contain nitrates, which open up blood vessels, reducing blood pressure and improving bloodflow, and decrease the amount of oxygen your muscles need during exercise. But stick with the real thing—cyclists who took a beetlike supplement instead still used less oxygen but didn't experience the same performance improvements.

Great things are done when men and mountains meet. This is not done by jostling in the street.

—WILLIAM BLAKE, poet

TiP
of the Week

DIY MASSAGE

Get a foam roller, and you can have the luxury of a daily post–ride massage for free. Rolling a muscle back and forth on a dense foam cylinder breaks down adhesions and scar tissue, warms and stretches muscles, increases circulation, and prevents soreness. Try rolling your hamstrings, glutes, quads, and calves back and forth slowly along the cylinder 10 to 12 times. Pause at tender spots, take a deep breath, and press your weight into them.

A bicycle ride is a flight from sadness.

—JAMES E. STARRS
The Literary Cyclist

MONDAY
ROUTE:

DISTANCE: | TIME:

NOTES:

CROSSTRAINING:

TUESDAY
ROUTE:

DISTANCE: | TIME:

NOTES:

CROSSTRAINING:

WEDNESDAY
ROUTE:

DISTANCE: | TIME:

NOTES:

CROSSTRAINING:

THURSDAY
ROUTE:

DISTANCE: | TIME:

NOTES:

CROSSTRAINING:

FRIDAY
ROUTE:

DISTANCE: | TIME:

NOTES:

CROSSTRAINING:

SATURDAY

ROUTE:

DISTANCE: TIME:

NOTES:

CROSSTRAINING:

SUNDAY

ROUTE:

DISTANCE: TIME:

NOTES:

CROSSTRAINING:

NOTES

WEEKLY TOTAL MILEAGE:

TOTAL MILEAGE TO DATE:

TRAINING

BUILD PACK SKILLS

Intimidated by group rides? Work with a buddy on trading pulls, riding closely side by side, and other basics. Not enough structure? Take a class. Many of the nation's velodromes offer beginner sessions. The tips you'll learn translate to the road. Visit www.racetra.com to find a track near you. Similarly, mountain biking and cyclocross improve balance and bike-handling techniques that will give you more confidence in a pack. Finally, find a shop ride with a no-drop policy.

TiP *of the Week*

RACE REHEARSAL

Getting ready for a big race? Preparing yourself mentally can be just as important as all those base miles you've logged. The night before, visualize how race day will go, then write down every detail. Is it dark when you get up? What are you wearing? What should you pack? What type of warmup will you do? What do your legs feel like? How's your breathing? Are you psyched up? Are you sitting or standing on climbs? Mentally rehearse every aspect before you fall asleep, and come race day, you'll have enough practice to almost ride on autopilot.

MONDAY

ROUTE:

DISTANCE: | TIME:

NOTES:

CROSSTRAINING:

TUESDAY

ROUTE:

DISTANCE: | TIME:

NOTES:

CROSSTRAINING:

WEDNESDAY

ROUTE:

DISTANCE: | TIME:

NOTES:

CROSSTRAINING:

THURSDAY

ROUTE:

DISTANCE: | TIME:

NOTES:

CROSSTRAINING:

FRIDAY

ROUTE:

DISTANCE: | TIME:

NOTES:

CROSSTRAINING:

SATURDAY

ROUTE:

DISTANCE: | TIME:

NOTES:

CROSSTRAINING:

SUNDAY

ROUTE:

DISTANCE: | TIME:

NOTES:

CROSSTRAINING:

NOTES

WEEKLY TOTAL MILEAGE:

TOTAL MILEAGE TO DATE:

Nutrition

STICK TO YOUR DIET PLAN

If you cave in to food cravings, don't try quitting junk cold turkey—make it harder to give in. Separate bags of chips or cookies into single servings. Or make problem foods less accessible. If ice cream is your weakness, don't bring it home. If you want it, you'll have to go get it. The point is to make yourself think before eating. And don't use good behavior as a reason to indulge—aim for healthier rewards instead, like new music on your iPod.

I thought of that while riding my bicycle.

—ALBERT EINSTEIN, on the Theory of Relativity

TiP
of the Week

RUN LIKE ROCKY

Stair running builds cardiovascular prowess and simulates the muscle action you need to crush steep climbs on your bike. Starting at the bottom of three or four flights of stairs, run up one step at a time as quickly as possible while maintaining good form—leaning slightly forward and lightly landing on and springing off the balls of your feet. Walk back down. Now head back up, taking two steps at a time. Then work up to three, if the steps aren't too steep. Repeat this sequence for 20 minutes twice a week.

Go confidently in the direction of your dreams. Live the life you have imagined.

—Henry David Thoreau

MONDAY

ROUTE:

DISTANCE: | TIME:

NOTES:

CROSSTRAINING:

TUESDAY

ROUTE:

DISTANCE: | TIME:

NOTES:

CROSSTRAINING:

WEDNESDAY

ROUTE:

DISTANCE: | TIME:

NOTES:

CROSSTRAINING:

THURSDAY

ROUTE:

DISTANCE: | TIME:

NOTES:

CROSSTRAINING:

FRIDAY

ROUTE:

DISTANCE: | TIME:

NOTES:

CROSSTRAINING:

SATURDAY

ROUTE:

DISTANCE: _____ TIME: _____

NOTES:

CROSSTRAINING:

SUNDAY

ROUTE:

DISTANCE: _____ TIME: _____

NOTES:

CROSSTRAINING:

NOTES

WEEKLY TOTAL MILEAGE:

TOTAL MILEAGE TO DATE:

TRAINING

MIX IT UP

Explore the woods on a mountain bike. Throw down in the local cyclocross race. Experimenting with different types of biking keeps you mentally fresh, boosts your skills, and reminds you that riding is fun.

TiP
of the Week

SWEET DREAMS

Up your slumber time, and you might be able to sprint faster. The body pumps out human growth hormone and regenerates during sleep, which means more speed—just one of the reasons pro racers swear by at least 8 hours of shut-eye and consider naps to be sacred.

Without ice cream there would be darkness and chaos.

—Don Kardong,
Olympic marathon
runner and author

MONDAY

ROUTE:

DISTANCE: | TIME:

NOTES:

CROSSTRAINING:

TUESDAY

ROUTE:

DISTANCE: | TIME:

NOTES:

CROSSTRAINING:

WEDNESDAY

ROUTE:

DISTANCE: | TIME:

NOTES:

CROSSTRAINING:

THURSDAY

ROUTE:

DISTANCE: | TIME:

NOTES:

CROSSTRAINING:

FRIDAY

ROUTE:

DISTANCE: | TIME:

NOTES:

CROSSTRAINING:

SATURDAY

ROUTE:

DISTANCE: | TIME:

NOTES:

CROSSTRAINING:

SUNDAY

ROUTE:

DISTANCE: | TIME:

NOTES:

CROSSTRAINING:

NOTES

WEEKLY TOTAL MILEAGE:

TOTAL MILEAGE TO DATE:

TRAINING

PLANK ON

Strengthen your core and improve your pedaling efficiency in just 3 minutes. Every morning before you start your day, hit the deck and do three plank poses.

1. Face down, propped up on your forearms and toes, body forming a straight line from head to heels.

2. Propped on your left forearm, placed perpendicular to your body, and the outside of your left foot, feet stacked, body in a straight diagonal line.

3. Propped on your right forearm and foot, same as Plank 2. Start with 20 to 30 seconds and work up to a minute.

TiP
of the Week

NEVER BONK

On long rides, it's easy to lose track of how much time has passed since you last ate or drank. One easy solution: Set a timer on your watch, smart-phone, or bike computer to go off at regular intervals. This can remind you to hydrate and fuel up as well as help train you to reach for your bottle or snack more regularly.

> *I firmly believe that any man's finest hour, the greatest fulfillment of all that he holds dear, is that moment when he has worked his heart out in a good cause and lies exhausted on the field of battle— victorious.*

—Vince Lombardi

MONDAY
ROUTE:

DISTANCE: | TIME:

NOTES:

CROSSTRAINING:

TUESDAY
ROUTE:

DISTANCE: | TIME:

NOTES:

CROSSTRAINING:

WEDNESDAY
ROUTE:

DISTANCE: | TIME:

NOTES:

CROSSTRAINING:

THURSDAY
ROUTE:

DISTANCE: | TIME:

NOTES:

CROSSTRAINING:

FRIDAY
ROUTE:

DISTANCE: | TIME:

NOTES:

CROSSTRAINING:

SATURDAY

ROUTE:

DISTANCE: TIME:

NOTES:

CROSSTRAINING:

SUNDAY

ROUTE:

DISTANCE: TIME:

NOTES:

CROSSTRAINING:

NOTES

WEEKLY TOTAL MILEAGE:

TOTAL MILEAGE TO DATE:

Maintenance

CHECK YOUR CHAIN

A dirty, stretched chain will ruin the rest of your drivetrain, so check your chain for wear every 1,000 miles or six months. Put it on the big chainring, then try to pull a single link off the ring. If you can see light between the chain and the ring, it's time for a new chain. Or purchase a chain-checking tool from Park or Rolhoff.

TiP
of the Week

CHOOSE HEALTHY FATS

Fat will help you ride longer, so you can burn more calories, and keep you fuller, so you don't binge on snack foods. Some healthy portions to shoot for:

• **Nuts and seeds:** Everything from pecans to pine nuts, almond butter to tahini. A serving size is 2 tablespoons.

• **Olives:** Black, green, mixed or blended in a spreadable tapenade. A serving is 10 large olives or 2 tablespoons of spread.

• **Oils:** Canola, flaxseed, peanut, safflower, walnut, sunflower, sesame, or olive. Cook with them; drizzle them; eat them in pesto. One serving is 1 tablespoon.

• **Avocado:** As guacamole or just slice and serve. One-quarter cup equals one serving.

• **Dark chocolate:** Go for one-quarter cup of dark or semisweet, or about 2 ounces.

MONDAY
ROUTE:

DISTANCE: | TIME:

NOTES:

CROSSTRAINING:

TUESDAY
ROUTE:

DISTANCE: | TIME:

NOTES:

CROSSTRAINING:

WEDNESDAY
ROUTE:

DISTANCE: | TIME:

NOTES:

CROSSTRAINING:

THURSDAY
ROUTE:

DISTANCE: | TIME:

NOTES:

CROSSTRAINING:

FRIDAY
ROUTE:

DISTANCE: | TIME:

NOTES:

CROSSTRAINING:

SATURDAY

ROUTE:

DISTANCE: | TIME:

NOTES:

CROSSTRAINING:

SUNDAY

ROUTE:

DISTANCE: | TIME:

NOTES:

CROSSTRAINING:

NOTES

WEEKLY TOTAL MILEAGE:

TOTAL MILEAGE TO DATE:

TRAINING

TACKLE HIGH ALTITUDES

Adjusting to high altitude takes a week, but days three and four—when your body is working overtime to increase red blood cells—are the most exhausting. If you're racing a one-day event, but don't have the luxury of taking seven days off, consider arriving just one night before. And always stay spinning: With less oxygen in the air for your muscles, you have less power to push big gears. Upshift and keep your cadence high to transfer the burden to your cardiovascular system.

When I go biking, I am mentally far, far away from civilization. The world is breaking someone else's heart.

—DIANE ACKERMAN, author and poet

TiP
of the Week

SHORT RIDES COUNT

No matter what the excuse—it's cold, you're tired, *Shark Week* is airing on the Discovery Channel—you can always shoehorn in a short ride. Head away from home for 30 minutes. If you're still miserable, turn around—you'll have logged an hour on the bike. Or, just keep riding. Something is better than nothing.

It never gets easier, you just go faster.

—GREG LEMOND

MONDAY

ROUTE:

DISTANCE: | TIME:

NOTES:

CROSSTRAINING:

TUESDAY

ROUTE:

DISTANCE: | TIME:

NOTES:

CROSSTRAINING:

WEDNESDAY

ROUTE:

DISTANCE: | TIME:

NOTES:

CROSSTRAINING:

THURSDAY

ROUTE:

DISTANCE: | TIME:

NOTES:

CROSSTRAINING:

FRIDAY

ROUTE:

DISTANCE: | TIME:

NOTES:

CROSSTRAINING:

SATURDAY

ROUTE:

DISTANCE: | TIME:

NOTES:

CROSSTRAINING:

SUNDAY

ROUTE:

DISTANCE: | TIME:

NOTES:

CROSSTRAINING:

NOTES

TRAINING

WALK IT OFF

At the end of a brutally difficult ride or race, don't collapse; instead, cool down. If you stop dead at the end of a ride, blood will pool in your extremities. That can leave you feeling light-headed, and you're more likely to feel soreness in your muscles the following day. Just 20 minutes of easy spinning or even walking will clean the blood and lactic acid from your legs and leave you feeling fresh the following day.

WEEKLY TOTAL MILEAGE:

TOTAL MILEAGE TO DATE:

TiP
of the Week

SUGAR HIGH

Sugar can wreak havoc on your diet and energy levels, but sometimes there's just no saying no to a sweet tooth. The key to keeping your sugar cravings balanced is timing. Eat your daily sweet in the context of a balanced meal, like after lunch. Because you'll already have food in your system to offset the sugar load, you're less likely to eat a whole sleeve of Thin Mints than if you'd waited until midafternoon, when your blood sugar is low and you're vulnerable to intense sugar cravings.

Ride as much or as little or as long or as short as you feel. But ride.

—EDDY MERCKX

MONDAY

ROUTE:

DISTANCE: | TIME:

NOTES:

CROSSTRAINING:

TUESDAY

ROUTE:

DISTANCE: | TIME:

NOTES:

CROSSTRAINING:

WEDNESDAY

ROUTE:

DISTANCE: | TIME:

NOTES:

CROSSTRAINING:

THURSDAY

ROUTE:

DISTANCE: | TIME:

NOTES:

CROSSTRAINING:

FRIDAY

ROUTE:

DISTANCE: | TIME:

NOTES:

CROSSTRAINING:

SATURDAY

ROUTE:

DISTANCE: | TIME:

NOTES:

CROSSTRAINING:

SUNDAY

ROUTE:

DISTANCE: | TIME:

NOTES:

CROSSTRAINING:

NOTES

_____
_____
_____
_____
_____
_____
_____
_____
_____
_____
_____
_____
_____
_____
_____

WEEKLY TOTAL MILEAGE:

TOTAL MILEAGE TO DATE:

TRAINING

TRAIN WITH A PURPOSE

Most riders spend too much time training. If you focus your riding based on the type of events that you're working for, you can highly specialize your training and reduce the amount of hours you spend in the saddle. If you're doing a mountain bike race that's under 2 hours, there's no reason to train for longer than 2 hours. In fact, you should focus all your training between 1 and 2 hours, working the anaerobic systems that fuel your most intense efforts.

TiP
of the Week

PICK ACTIVE CALORIES

One-quarter to one-third of your meal should consist of active and semi-active calories from protein. One-half should be active calories from fruits and vegetables. One-quarter should be active and semi-active calories from whole grain starches. Save couch potato calories for occasional indulgences and snacks.

Active Calories
- Lean meat, fish, poultry
- Fruits
- Vegetables
- Whole grains
- Beans, legumes, and soy foods

Semi-Active Calories
- Fiber-rich cereal
- Whole grain bread
- Low-fat dairy
- Potatoes
- Soups

Couch Potato Calories
- Pastries, cookies, pies, cakes
- Fatty processed meats
- Chips, pretzels, snack foods

MONDAY
ROUTE:

DISTANCE: | TIME:

NOTES:

CROSSTRAINING:

TUESDAY
ROUTE:

DISTANCE: | TIME:

NOTES:

CROSSTRAINING:

WEDNESDAY
ROUTE:

DISTANCE: | TIME:

NOTES:

CROSSTRAINING:

THURSDAY
ROUTE:

DISTANCE: | TIME:

NOTES:

CROSSTRAINING:

FRIDAY
ROUTE:

DISTANCE: | TIME:

NOTES:

CROSSTRAINING:

SATURDAY

ROUTE:

DISTANCE: TIME:

NOTES:

CROSSTRAINING:

SUNDAY

ROUTE:

DISTANCE: TIME:

NOTES:

CROSSTRAINING:

NOTES

WEEKLY TOTAL MILEAGE:

TOTAL MILEAGE TO DATE:

TRAINING

STAY SALTED

• **2,400:** Maximum daily recommended milligrams of sodium

• **1,000:** Milligrams of sodium you should replace—via high-sodium sports drinks, energy foods, or supplements (such as endurolytes and lava salts)—each hour when riding more than 4 hours if you're a salty sweater (i.e., you typically crust your kit)

SOURCE: *Monique Ryan, RD, LDN, author of* Sports Nutrition for Endurance Athletes, *2nd edition*

I refuse to let myself ride in a comfort zone, as if I have nothing more to prove and can slow down.

—JENS VOIGT, on continuing to race at 39

TiP
of the Week

ZERO IN

Having trouble getting your bike to go exactly where you want it to on the trail? Try the following: Look about 10 feet down the trail and zero in on exactly where you want your front tire to go—not the millions of places you don't want it to go. This will help you nail just the right line every time.

Bicycle racing has two kinds of winners: those who win races, and those who win our hearts.

—JAMES STARTT, author of *Tour de France/Tour de Force*

MONDAY

ROUTE:

DISTANCE: | TIME:

NOTES:

CROSSTRAINING:

TUESDAY

ROUTE:

DISTANCE: | TIME:

NOTES:

CROSSTRAINING:

WEDNESDAY

ROUTE:

DISTANCE: | TIME:

NOTES:

CROSSTRAINING:

THURSDAY

ROUTE:

DISTANCE: | TIME:

NOTES:

CROSSTRAINING:

FRIDAY

ROUTE:

DISTANCE: | TIME:

NOTES:

CROSSTRAINING:

SATURDAY

ROUTE:

DISTANCE: | TIME:

NOTES:

CROSSTRAINING:

SUNDAY

ROUTE:

DISTANCE: | TIME:

NOTES:

CROSSTRAINING:

NOTES

WEEKLY TOTAL MILEAGE:

TOTAL MILEAGE TO DATE:

TRAINING

PREVENT CRAMPS

Cramps seem to be as much a part of cycling as flat tires and sore backsides. Yet, it doesn't have to be so. Here's how to prevent skeletal muscle cramps on your next ride.

• **Adequate hydration:** Dehydration causes cramping. Stay adequately hydrated, and you should be in the clear.

• **Electrolyte replacement:** Maintaining the proper level of magnesium, potassium, sodium, and chloride in your system is also important in the prevention of cramps.

• **Regular stretching:** Before and after rides, stretching—although not proven to be a cure-all for cramping—is a good preventive measure.

• **Proper training:** Mimicking the intensity, distance, and style of ride that you are preparing for will go a long way in the prevention of cramps.

TiP
of the Week

WHERE THE CARBS ARE

Fruits and vegetables are a healthier and more substantial source of carbohydrate than most people realize.

- Succotash, cooked (1 cup), 47g
- Sweet potato, baked, with skin (1 large), 44g
- Raisins, seedless (¼ cup), 32g
- Banana (1 medium), 30g
- Squash, winter, cooked (1 cup), 30g
- Peas, cooked (1 cup), 25g
- Peach (1 large), 17g
- Cantaloupe (1 cup), 15g
- Orange (1 medium), 14g

Compare with pasta and grains:

- Long-grain white rice (1 cup), 45g
- Tagliatelle (1 cup), 44g
- Spaghetti (1 cup), 40g
- Short-grain white rice (1 cup), 37g
- Spaghetti, whole wheat (1 cup), 37g
- Pita bread, white (6-inch diameter), 33g
- French bread (5 inches), 18g
- Wheat bread (1 slice), 12g

MONDAY
ROUTE:

DISTANCE: | TIME:

NOTES:

CROSSTRAINING:

TUESDAY
ROUTE:

DISTANCE: | TIME:

NOTES:

CROSSTRAINING:

WEDNESDAY
ROUTE:

DISTANCE: | TIME:

NOTES:

CROSSTRAINING:

THURSDAY
ROUTE:

DISTANCE: | TIME:

NOTES:

CROSSTRAINING:

FRIDAY
ROUTE:

DISTANCE: | TIME:

NOTES:

CROSSTRAINING:

SATURDAY

ROUTE:

DISTANCE: | TIME:

NOTES:

CROSSTRAINING:

SUNDAY

ROUTE:

DISTANCE: | TIME:

NOTES:

CROSSTRAINING:

NOTES

TRAINING

SHRINK YOUR CYCLING CIRCLE

Group rides are great for improving fitness and teaching you to hold a steady line, but it can be easy to loaf in the middle of a large pack and expend only a fraction of the power put out by the usual leaders. Find a small group to train with once or twice a week so you're forced to take the lead.

The bicycle is a curious vehicle. Its passenger is its engine.

—JOHN HOWARD, Olympic cyclist

WEEKLY TOTAL MILEAGE:

TOTAL MILEAGE TO DATE:

TiP
of the Week

SPICE REVS METABOLISM

Rev up the spice in your food, and the capsaicin in hot peppers may trigger protein changes in your body that stimulate weight loss and fight fat storage, reports a 2010 study. Plus new research finds that consuming spicy food can also raise your metabolism and help keep weight off better than dieting.

I did everything to win races, but without luck, I wouldn't be where I am.

—STEPHEN ROCHE, winner of the 1987 Tour de France and Tour of Italy

MONDAY

ROUTE:

DISTANCE: | TIME:

NOTES:

CROSSTRAINING:

TUESDAY

ROUTE:

DISTANCE: | TIME:

NOTES:

CROSSTRAINING:

WEDNESDAY

ROUTE:

DISTANCE: | TIME:

NOTES:

CROSSTRAINING:

THURSDAY

ROUTE:

DISTANCE: | TIME:

NOTES:

CROSSTRAINING:

FRIDAY

ROUTE:

DISTANCE: | TIME:

NOTES:

CROSSTRAINING:

SATURDAY

ROUTE:

DISTANCE: | TIME:

NOTES:

CROSSTRAINING:

SUNDAY

ROUTE:

DISTANCE: | TIME:

NOTES:

CROSSTRAINING:

NOTES

WEEKLY TOTAL MILEAGE:

TOTAL MILEAGE TO DATE:

TRAINING

HIT REFRESH

Take 3 or 4 days off the bike, and you may actually come back faster and stronger. After a week or more, however, you lose about 2 to 4 percent of your fitness per week. If you know in advance you're in for a layoff, do short but intense efforts to forestall losses— a half hour of exercise is all it takes to maintain cycling fitness and muscle memory.

TiP
of the Week

KEEP YOUR KIT IN ROTATION

When the cold wind is whipping, it's tempting to slip into sweats. But beware: Get too comfortable and you'll forget what's under the hoodie. Scientists at Cornell University found that prison inmates gained an average of 20 to 25 pounds 6 months into incarceration in part because of their baggy orange jumpsuits. The researchers recommend keeping the clothes you associate with being fit in plain view year-round. Make this tip more effective: Don't just look at your kit, ride in it.

The way to gain a good reputation is to endeavor to be what you desire to appear.

—SOCRATES

MONDAY

ROUTE:

DISTANCE: | TIME:

NOTES:

CROSSTRAINING:

TUESDAY

ROUTE:

DISTANCE: | TIME:

NOTES:

CROSSTRAINING:

WEDNESDAY

ROUTE:

DISTANCE: | TIME:

NOTES:

CROSSTRAINING:

THURSDAY

ROUTE:

DISTANCE: | TIME:

NOTES:

CROSSTRAINING:

FRIDAY

ROUTE:

DISTANCE: | TIME:

NOTES:

CROSSTRAINING:

SATURDAY

ROUTE:

DISTANCE: _____ TIME: _____

NOTES:

CROSSTRAINING:

SUNDAY

ROUTE:

DISTANCE: _____ TIME: _____

NOTES:

CROSSTRAINING:

NOTES

WEEKLY TOTAL MILEAGE:

TOTAL MILEAGE TO DATE:

TRAINING

INSIDER TRAINING

Riding indoors on a trainer doesn't have to be dull—and it can put you on the fast track to fitness. Start by spinning easy for 10 to 15 minutes before each workout. Then, instead of pedaling as fast as you can until boredom sets in, try four 1-minute fast-pedal intervals in an easy gear with as high a cadence as possible. Keep your rate of perceived exertion low, and recover for 2 minutes between efforts. Then pedal 5 minutes easy before repeating the fast-pedal interval, making the resistance slightly harder this time. Continue for the duration of your workout, and finish the session with a 10-minute cooldown.

TiP
of the Week

DRY YOUR SHOES

After a wet ride, the best way to dry your shoes is to stuff them with wadded newspaper. The paper will pull the water from the soggy material and help your shoes maintain the proper shape. Remove the paper after 8 to 10 hours. Repeat if necessary.

Motivation is what gets you started. Habit is what keeps you going.

—JIM RYUN, record-setting track athlete

MONDAY
ROUTE:

DISTANCE: | TIME:

NOTES:

CROSSTRAINING:

TUESDAY
ROUTE:

DISTANCE: | TIME:

NOTES:

CROSSTRAINING:

WEDNESDAY
ROUTE:

DISTANCE: | TIME:

NOTES:

CROSSTRAINING:

THURSDAY
ROUTE:

DISTANCE: | TIME:

NOTES:

CROSSTRAINING:

FRIDAY
ROUTE:

DISTANCE: | TIME:

NOTES:

CROSSTRAINING:

SATURDAY

ROUTE:

DISTANCE: | TIME:

NOTES:

CROSSTRAINING:

SUNDAY

ROUTE:

DISTANCE: | TIME:

NOTES:

CROSSTRAINING:

NOTES

WEEKLY TOTAL MILEAGE:

TOTAL MILEAGE TO DATE:

TRAINING

CROSSTRAIN: KETTLEBELL POWER

Twenty minutes with a kettlebell is all it takes to boost aerobic fitness and build up key cycling muscles in your hips, core, legs, and arms. Try this full-body move, using a 5- to 10-pound weight to start: Stand with feet apart, holding a kettlebell in front of you. With your back straight, press down into a squat. Swing the kettlebell back through your legs. Stand and press hips forward, swinging the weight to chest level. Do three sets of 10 to 15 reps, and say goodbye to up to 272 calories.

TiP
of the Week

BLAST OFF THE POUNDS

When you hit the weights this winter, use explosive movements instead of slow resistance exercises to fry calories and avoid fatigue. Studies have shown slow reps only fatigue muscles, but explosive muscle contractions expend more energy and increase weight loss.

I say, 'Shut up, legs!'

—JENS VOIGT, on how he copes with pain

MONDAY

ROUTE:

DISTANCE: | TIME:

NOTES:

CROSSTRAINING:

TUESDAY

ROUTE:

DISTANCE: | TIME:

NOTES:

CROSSTRAINING:

WEDNESDAY

ROUTE:

DISTANCE: | TIME:

NOTES:

CROSSTRAINING:

THURSDAY

ROUTE:

DISTANCE: | TIME:

NOTES:

CROSSTRAINING:

FRIDAY

ROUTE:

DISTANCE: | TIME:

NOTES:

CROSSTRAINING:

SATURDAY

ROUTE:

DISTANCE: TIME:

NOTES:

CROSSTRAINING:

SUNDAY

ROUTE:

DISTANCE: TIME:

NOTES:

CROSSTRAINING:

NOTES

_____
_____
_____
_____
_____
_____
_____
_____
_____
_____
_____
_____
_____

WEEKLY TOTAL MILEAGE:

TOTAL MILEAGE TO DATE:

TRAINING

SNOW SEASON

For winter crosstraining— or when the weather is more conducive to making snow angels than cycling—try snow-shoeing, which detonates 550 calories an hour and builds cardiovascular fitness. Your quads will send off that familiar singe as you head uphill because the lower-body range of motion is very similar to pedaling a bike.

TiP
of the Week

PACK SAFETY

Riding in a pack feels good for many reasons—camaraderie, training, hiding from the wind. But clusters of cyclists can irritate other road users, to the point that some communities try to regulate group rides. Here are a few tips to keep your pack safe and free from scrutiny.

• **Ride single file or two abreast,** depending on the law in your state.

• **Follow all traffic laws.** Signal turns and don't blow through stop signs.

• **As tempting as it is, don't pass slow-moving traffic on the right.** It's illegal in most states, and you could easily ride into the path of a right-turning car. Instead, pass on the left (if there's a passing lane) or get in line behind them.

• **Try to keep any conversations with drivers civil,** even if the motorist is in the wrong.

MONDAY

ROUTE:

DISTANCE: | TIME:

NOTES:

CROSSTRAINING:

TUESDAY

ROUTE:

DISTANCE: | TIME:

NOTES:

CROSSTRAINING:

WEDNESDAY

ROUTE:

DISTANCE: | TIME:

NOTES:

CROSSTRAINING:

THURSDAY

ROUTE:

DISTANCE: | TIME:

NOTES:

CROSSTRAINING:

FRIDAY

ROUTE:

DISTANCE: | TIME:

NOTES:

CROSSTRAINING:

SATURDAY

ROUTE:

DISTANCE: | TIME:

NOTES:

CROSSTRAINING:

SUNDAY

ROUTE:

DISTANCE: | TIME:

NOTES:

CROSSTRAINING:

NOTES

WEEKLY TOTAL MILEAGE:

TOTAL MILEAGE TO DATE:

Nutrition

EAT WINTER FRESH

Cool weather doesn't mean mining the frozen-foods aisle for produce: Plenty of winter vegetables are heartier, more filling, and even more satisfying than their summer counterparts. Winter veggies can also contribute postride carbohydrates to replace glycogen stores and jump-start recovery. Try sweet potatoes, Brussels sprouts, leeks, broccoli raab, kale, parsnips, snow peas, or winter squash.

Anything is possible. You can be told that you have a 90 percent chance or a 50 percent chance or a 1 percent chance, but you have to believe, and you have to fight.

—LANCE ARMSTRONG

TiP
of the Week

TRUE YOUR WHEEL

To restore a smooth roll to your wheel, spin it and locate the section that is wobbling toward one side. On that side of the wheel, use a spoke wrench to loosen the two spokes closest to the wobble one-quarter turn. On the other side of the wheel, tighten the two closest spokes one-quarter turn. (Which way is tight and which is loose? Imagine the tire and tube are gone and you are standing behind the mounted wheel—front or rear—looking at the spokes and nipples through the rim. Turning the nipple clockwise tightens the spoke, counterclockwise loosens it.) Spin the wheel and tune the wobble again. Never turn the nipples more than a quarter-turn at a time, and be prepared to work back and forth, loosening or tightening several times on each side until the wheel spins true.

MONDAY

ROUTE:

DISTANCE: | TIME:

NOTES:

CROSSTRAINING:

TUESDAY

ROUTE:

DISTANCE: | TIME:

NOTES:

CROSSTRAINING:

WEDNESDAY

ROUTE:

DISTANCE: | TIME:

NOTES:

CROSSTRAINING:

THURSDAY

ROUTE:

DISTANCE: | TIME:

NOTES:

CROSSTRAINING:

FRIDAY

ROUTE:

DISTANCE: | TIME:

NOTES:

CROSSTRAINING:

SATURDAY

ROUTE:

DISTANCE: | TIME:

NOTES:

CROSSTRAINING:

SUNDAY

ROUTE:

DISTANCE: | TIME:

NOTES:

CROSSTRAINING:

NOTES

WEEKLY TOTAL MILEAGE:

TOTAL MILEAGE TO DATE:

TRAINING

BECOME AN INCREDIBLE SPRINTER AND BIKE HANDLER

Riding and racing on any one of the more than two dozen velodromes in the United States will fine-tune your sprint, buff up your muscles, and hone your bike handling. With no brakes and only one gear, training and racing on the track is a time-honored method for rounding out a racer's fitness and skills, but it can help anyone become a better cyclist.

As long as I breathe, I attack.

—BERNARD HINAULT, five-time Tour de France winner

NOW WHAT?

There's an entire year of experience in this log. What can it tell you?

Welcome to the end of your *Bicycling Training Journal*. Have you spent the past year compiling a detailed riding log? Did you record a lot of hard numbers? Or did you concentrate on how riding made you feel and where you'd like to ride in the future?

No matter what you've chronicled, it'd be a pity to stick the journal on a shelf or file it away when you could be using it to plot your riding plans and goals for next year. Sift through these pages. Learn what type of riding is important to you. You'll find it easier to set attainable goals and build resolve when you study where you've been and what you've done.

Here are a few pointers for using your completed journal to boost next year's performance.

1. Look back at the best rides of the year. What made them so incredible? Was it the location? A particular group of riding partners? A certain distance? Try to trace a common thread through your great riding experiences and repeat them in the future.

2. Try to discover what time of day your body responds the best to exercise. We all have a few hours every day when our body performs at its peak. Figure out when that is, and try to get out on your bike during that time.

3. In reviewing your journal, you'll remember rides that you loved and wonder "Why didn't I do them more often?" Find three rides that worked for you, and pencil them into your journal for next year.

4. Sift through the data, and find the month when you were able to ride the greatest number of hours. What was working for you? Were you buckling down and making time to ride? Was it that there was more daylight? Was it a slow time at work? Discover and exploit your peak performance seasons.

5. Review the periods that you rode the least. What was keeping you from getting out more? Was it a major life event or simply a time management issue? Is there a way that you can better organize your life to make more time for riding?

6. Did you suffer any hard-to-explain injuries last year? Your diary will probably contain clues to the origin of your problem. Was it that you rode too hard when you were lacking fitness? Did a seemingly small injury lead to bigger problems? Was it the result of stress and exhaustion?

7. Based on what you've logged in your journal and the memories it stirs, make a plan for the coming year. Include short-term goals (such as a day of the week that you'll always make time to ride) and longer-term dreams (an event that you want to focus on, a cycling-oriented vacation, etc.).

8. Based on the experience reflected in your journal, pick rides, races, or other events that you want to enter next year. Perhaps it's an event where you've done well and want to repeat that performance. Maybe it's something you've always dreamed of doing, like a 24-hour race or a double century.

RAVE RIDES

More than anything else, this is the section you'll enjoy reading later when you're having trouble finding motivation.

Whether you took a scenic spin along the Oregon coast, tackled your first century ride, or checked a cross-country bike tour off your bucket list, you'll want to remember this year's "all-time greatest rides." That's why we've included this section. Throughout the year, take notes on the rides you took, the goals met, and the lessons learned. The shortcut you found in your morning commute. The time you outsprinted your fastest buddy. The new trail you found while cruising around the woods behind your house. You think you'll remember these moments forever, but as the rave rides start to accumulate, details and time frames start to blur. Get them all down to enjoy the memories for years to come.

RAVE RIDES

RIDE NAME _____ DATE _____

RIDING PARTNERS _____

DISTANCE _____ LENGTH OF TIME _____

START LOCATION _____

ROUTE DESCRIPTION _____

BIGGEST CHALLENGE _____

MOST MEMORABLE MOMENT _____

_____

RAVE RIDES

RIDE NAME _____ DATE _____

RIDING PARTNERS _____

DISTANCE _____ LENGTH OF TIME _____

START LOCATION _____

ROUTE DESCRIPTION _____

BIGGEST CHALLENGE _____

MOST MEMORABLE MOMENT _____

_____

RAVE RIDES

RIDE NAME _____ DATE _____

RIDING PARTNERS _____

DISTANCE _____ LENGTH OF TIME _____

START LOCATION _____

ROUTE DESCRIPTION _____

BIGGEST CHALLENGE _____

MOST MEMORABLE MOMENT _____

_____

RAVE RIDES

RIDE NAME _____ DATE _____

RIDING PARTNERS _____

DISTANCE _____ LENGTH OF TIME _____

START LOCATION _____

ROUTE DESCRIPTION _____

BIGGEST CHALLENGE _____

MOST MEMORABLE MOMENT _____

_____

RAVE RIDES

RIDE NAME _____ DATE _____

RIDING PARTNERS _____

DISTANCE _____ LENGTH OF TIME _____

START LOCATION _____

ROUTE DESCRIPTION _____

BIGGEST CHALLENGE _____

MOST MEMORABLE MOMENT _____

_____

RAVE RIDES

RIDE NAME _____ DATE _____

RIDING PARTNERS _____

DISTANCE _____ LENGTH OF TIME _____

START LOCATION _____

ROUTE DESCRIPTION _____

BIGGEST CHALLENGE _____

MOST MEMORABLE MOMENT _____

_____

RAVE RIDES

RIDE NAME _____ DATE _____

RIDING PARTNERS _____

DISTANCE _____ LENGTH OF TIME _____

START LOCATION _____

ROUTE DESCRIPTION _____

BIGGEST CHALLENGE _____

MOST MEMORABLE MOMENT _____

_____

RAVE RIDES

RIDE NAME _____ DATE _____

RIDING PARTNERS _____

DISTANCE _____ LENGTH OF TIME _____

START LOCATION _____

ROUTE DESCRIPTION _____

BIGGEST CHALLENGE _____

MOST MEMORABLE MOMENT _____

_____

RAVE RIDES

RIDE NAME _____ DATE _____

RIDING PARTNERS _____

DISTANCE _____ LENGTH OF TIME _____

START LOCATION _____

ROUTE DESCRIPTION _____

BIGGEST CHALLENGE _____

MOST MEMORABLE MOMENT _____

_____

RAVE RIDES

RIDE NAME _____ DATE _____

RIDING PARTNERS _____

DISTANCE _____ LENGTH OF TIME _____

START LOCATION _____

ROUTE DESCRIPTION _____

BIGGEST CHALLENGE _____

MOST MEMORABLE MOMENT _____

_____

RAVE RIDES

RIDE NAME _____ DATE _____

RIDING PARTNERS _____

DISTANCE _____ LENGTH OF TIME _____

START LOCATION _____

ROUTE DESCRIPTION _____

BIGGEST CHALLENGE _____

MOST MEMORABLE MOMENT _____

_____

RAVE RIDES

RIDE NAME _____ DATE _____

RIDING PARTNERS _____

DISTANCE _____ LENGTH OF TIME _____

START LOCATION _____

ROUTE DESCRIPTION _____

BIGGEST CHALLENGE _____

MOST MEMORABLE MOMENT _____

_____

RAVE RIDES

RIDE NAME _____ DATE _____

RIDING PARTNERS _____

DISTANCE _____ LENGTH OF TIME _____

START LOCATION _____

ROUTE DESCRIPTION _____

BIGGEST CHALLENGE _____

MOST MEMORABLE MOMENT _____

_____

RAVE RIDES

RIDE NAME _____ DATE _____

RIDING PARTNERS _____

DISTANCE _____ LENGTH OF TIME _____

START LOCATION _____

ROUTE DESCRIPTION _____

BIGGEST CHALLENGE _____

MOST MEMORABLE MOMENT _____

_____

RAVE RIDES

RIDE NAME _____ DATE _____

RIDING PARTNERS _____

DISTANCE _____ LENGTH OF TIME _____

START LOCATION _____

ROUTE DESCRIPTION _____

BIGGEST CHALLENGE _____

MOST MEMORABLE MOMENT _____

_____

RACE PERFORMANCE

Time to hone in on your toughest competitor: you. As much as racing is about having one eye on the podium and the other on your main rival, your primary motivation for pinning on a number will likely be to find out just how fast and furious you're capable of riding. Track your performance, placements, and times to see the real progress that comes from pushing yourself in competition. Analyze the results with the intensity of a football coach huddled over next week's game plan, or simply glance through old races to remember just how often you sprinted to a finish line. But don't beat yourself up if you have a bad day in the velodrome or on the course. Lightning speed and improved technique is something to hone over the long haul, and even pros face setbacks. In the wise words of Greg LeMond, "It doesn't get easier, you just get faster." How fast are you getting? Keep track of it here.

RACE PERFORMANCE

RIDE NAME _____

TOWN _____ DISTANCE _____

COURSE DESCRIPTION _____

YOUR TIME _____

YOUR PLACE OVERALL _____

AGE GROUP PLACE _____

DESCRIBE THE WHOLE EXPERIENCE _____

RACE PERFORMANCE

RIDE NAME _____

TOWN _____ DISTANCE _____

COURSE DESCRIPTION _____

YOUR TIME _____

YOUR PLACE OVERALL _____

AGE GROUP PLACE _____

DESCRIBE THE WHOLE EXPERIENCE _____

_____

RACE PERFORMANCE

RIDE NAME _____

TOWN _____ DISTANCE _____

COURSE DESCRIPTION _____

YOUR TIME _____

YOUR PLACE OVERALL _____

AGE GROUP PLACE _____

DESCRIBE THE WHOLE EXPERIENCE _____

_____

RACE PERFORMANCE

RIDE NAME _____

TOWN _____ DISTANCE _____

COURSE DESCRIPTION _____

YOUR TIME _____

YOUR PLACE OVERALL _____

AGE GROUP PLACE _____

DESCRIBE THE WHOLE EXPERIENCE _____

_____

RACE PERFORMANCE

RIDE NAME _____

TOWN _____ DISTANCE _____

COURSE DESCRIPTION _____

YOUR TIME _____

YOUR PLACE OVERALL _____

AGE GROUP PLACE _____

DESCRIBE THE WHOLE EXPERIENCE _____

_____

RACE PERFORMANCE

RIDE NAME _____

TOWN _____ DISTANCE _____

COURSE DESCRIPTION _____

YOUR TIME _____

YOUR PLACE OVERALL _____

AGE GROUP PLACE _____

DESCRIBE THE WHOLE EXPERIENCE _____

_____

RACE PERFORMANCE

RIDE NAME _____

TOWN _____ DISTANCE _____

COURSE DESCRIPTION _____

YOUR TIME _____

YOUR PLACE OVERALL _____

AGE GROUP PLACE _____

DESCRIBE THE WHOLE EXPERIENCE _____

_____

RACE PERFORMANCE

RIDE NAME _____

TOWN _____ DISTANCE _____

COURSE DESCRIPTION _____

YOUR TIME _____

YOUR PLACE OVERALL _____

AGE GROUP PLACE _____

DESCRIBE THE WHOLE EXPERIENCE _____

_____

RACE PERFORMANCE

RIDE NAME _____

TOWN _____ DISTANCE _____

COURSE DESCRIPTION _____

YOUR TIME _____

YOUR PLACE OVERALL _____

AGE GROUP PLACE _____

DESCRIBE THE WHOLE EXPERIENCE _____

_____

RACE PERFORMANCE

RIDE NAME _____

TOWN _____ DISTANCE _____

COURSE DESCRIPTION _____

YOUR TIME _____

YOUR PLACE OVERALL _____

AGE GROUP PLACE _____

DESCRIBE THE WHOLE EXPERIENCE _____

_____

RACE PERFORMANCE

RIDE NAME _____

TOWN _____ DISTANCE _____

COURSE DESCRIPTION _____

YOUR TIME _____

YOUR PLACE OVERALL _____

AGE GROUP PLACE _____

DESCRIBE THE WHOLE EXPERIENCE _____

_____

RACE PERFORMANCE

RIDE NAME _____

TOWN _____ DISTANCE _____

COURSE DESCRIPTION _____

YOUR TIME _____

YOUR PLACE OVERALL _____

AGE GROUP PLACE _____

DESCRIBE THE WHOLE EXPERIENCE _____

_____

RACE PERFORMANCE

RIDE NAME _____

TOWN _____ DISTANCE _____

COURSE DESCRIPTION _____

YOUR TIME _____

YOUR PLACE OVERALL _____

AGE GROUP PLACE _____

DESCRIBE THE WHOLE EXPERIENCE _____

_____

RACE PERFORMANCE

RIDE NAME _____

TOWN _____ DISTANCE _____

COURSE DESCRIPTION _____

YOUR TIME _____

YOUR PLACE OVERALL _____

AGE GROUP PLACE _____

DESCRIBE THE WHOLE EXPERIENCE _____

_____

RACE PERFORMANCE

RIDE NAME _____

TOWN _____ DISTANCE _____

COURSE DESCRIPTION _____

YOUR TIME _____

YOUR PLACE OVERALL _____

AGE GROUP PLACE _____

DESCRIBE THE WHOLE EXPERIENCE _____

_____

HIT THE DIRT

Who says a road bike belongs only on the pavement? Whether you venture onto the dirt or the pavé, taking those skinny tires off-road can turn just a regular ride into something far more memorable. Plus, you'll improve your handling skills along with your fitness, says Michael Gibbons, a coach at Cadence Cycling & Multisport Centers in Philadelphia. Use his tips to prep your bike and body, then go find some of the rough stuff.

Gear Up

WHEELS AND TIRES Forget the carbon clinchers: A more durable alloy box-section rim will dampen vibration from the uneven surface. To maximize comfort and traction, use the widest tires your frame will permit—at least 25mm. Allow a little space between the tire and the frame in case your wheel goes slightly out of true.

CLOTHING A cycling cap and sunglasses protect eyes from dust and debris. Consider adding spandex booties to keep kicked-up grit from lodging in shoes.
EXTRA FOOD You burn more calories off-road because of the increased demands on your body. Aim to take in at least 250 calories an hour.

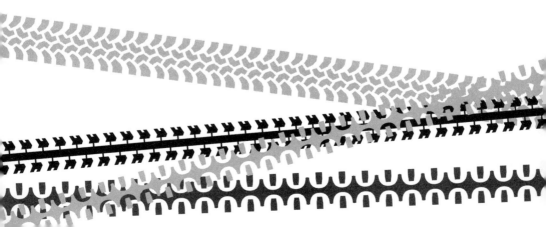

Perfect Your Form

EYES Look where you want to ride and your bike will follow—don't fixate on ruts and other obstacles.

UPPER BODY Keep hands, arms, shoulders, and neck relaxed. Visualize the bike bouncing around while your core remains motionless. Bend your elbows slightly more than usual for additional shock absorption.

HANDS Experiment with hand positions: Move from the brake hoods to the bar top to the drops and find where you feel most comfortable. For extra control when things get really rough, use the drops.

LOWER BODY Hover over the saddle to let the bike flow beneath you (and reduce the impact on your sensitive spots). Peek down at your toes once in a while to make sure they're pointed straight: Where the ankles go, the knees follow, and flailing knees waste energy, send the bike off line, and may even set you up for injury. But don't lock your knees or ankles—this will make the bike harder to control.

COMMUTE
BY BIKE

You can maximize your commute by turning it into a training ride as well, says Quinn Keogh, a rider for Team Exergy and former coach who utilizes this strategy when traveling to college classes in Portland, Oregon. Here's how.

1. **Start with realistic goals,** which may include riding 2 days a week or using a combination of public transportation and the bike.

2. **Map out three routes ahead of time:** short (the safest direct path), medium, and long (add some hills or a detour on a scenic trail). Plan to take each on specific days, but you can always revert to the short one as needed.

3. **Build in time for a warmup and cooldown**—easy pedaling for 5 minutes at each end of short routes; 15 for longer ones.

4. **Use stops to your advantage.** Think of red lights, stop signs, and traffic as mini recovery periods, but try to include one section with few stops on your longer routes.

5. **Aim to drink one bottle of water per hour of riding.** When you arrive, hydrate and eat a snack that includes carbs and protein—such as an apple and string cheese—which will give you energy to focus throughout the day.

GET THE WET OUT

Caught in a downpour?
Use this post-ride ritual to prolong the life of your bike.

RINSE CYCLE Before taking cover, hose down your bike using low pressure—if it's too high, you could force grit into internal components such as the bottom bracket, hubs, and bearings, or wash away necessary lubricants. Don't forget wheels, drivetrain, and braking surfaces—parts on which road crud accumulates.

SPIN CYCLE Remove your seatpost and turn your bike upside down so water can escape. Even if your frame is carbon, which can't rust, do it to ensure no moisture sits in your bottom bracket. Then take off your wheels. If they have a drain hole, lay them at an angle that lets the water run out of the opening. No drain holes? Deflate your tires and drain water through the valve-stem hole.

DRY CYCLE Move the whole operation out of the rain, then replace your wheels and seatpost. Run a clean, dry towel over your entire bike, getting into all the nooks and crannies. Your final step: Lube the chain (see how at bicycling.com/howtolube).

BIKE FIT BASICS
A Bike That Doesn't Fit Is No Bike at All

If your bike doesn't fit you, it's never going to feel like your bike. Finding a comfortable riding position that maximizes your power will do more to ensure you return to your saddle regularly (and happily!) than any other factor in your training plan.

Proper bike fit isn't an absolute, and from one season to the next you might need to make slight adjustments to your settings and position. Use the information below to get started and find your ideal position, and continue to make slight adjustments from there. And if you need more assistance, don't be afraid to consult your local bike shop.

Seat

HEIGHT: Theories vary on the correct calculation for seat height, but most experts agree that your leg should be nearly straight but not locked or stretched as you hit the bottom of the pedal stroke. A more scientific way to generate a beginning number for the distance between the top of your saddle and the platform of your pedal is to carefully measure your inseam and multiply it by 0.883.

FORE AND AFT: Sitting on your bike, pedal backward a few rotations, and stop with your cranks parallel to the ground. Drop a plumb line (a weighted string) from the bony bump just below your kneecap down to your foot. In the proper position, it should sit on top of the pedal axle or be less than 5mm fore or aft of it.

ANGLE: With your bike on a flat surface, use a small level to determine an absolutely level position for the saddle. Experiment from there. A very slight tilt in either direction can dramatically alter the pressure you feel as you sit.

Handlebar

HEIGHT AND REACH: The rule of thumb for handlebar reach on a road bike is that your arms should form a 90-degree angle with your torso when your hands are on the hoods. Mountain bike riders should be positioned so that there is less room between their torso and arms.

WIDTH: Handlebar width is directly related to shoulder width. Road cyclists should choose a bar that is as wide as their shoulders, measured as the distance between the bony bumps on the outside top of the shoulder joints. Mountain bike riders should select a bar that suits the terrain they ride most often—go narrow for singletrack, wider for fire roads.

ANGLE: Whether mountain or road, this is nearly all personal choice. Start with a neutral position and experiment from there. During your experiment, don't just change the angle of your bar; change the angle and position of your controls.

Cleats

FORE AND AFT: Your cleats should be mounted so that the pedal spindles sit directly under the ball of your foot.

LATERAL: Riders who are using clipless pedals for the first time should be sure to use a system with cleats that have float. This allows the heel of the foot to swivel both in and out, allowing you to find the best lateral alignment for your foot.

BIKE SETUP RECORD

Consider this your little black book of bicycling.

We've all had our great loves, but ultimately bikes come and bikes go. Before you know it, the Trek you doted on last season will be collecting dust in your garage, and you'll be cranking out the miles on a sleek and sexy Litespeed. Eventually, you'll sell that one and buy a dream bike with a more exotic pedigree. A little Italian number perhaps? On and on, the cycle of cycles continues.

Once your current bike is perfectly configured, we suggest that you use these pages to record as much information about it as possible. Not only will this make the transition to a new bike easier, but also it'll help in 5 or 6 years when you're dreaming wistfully of the way your old Litespeed fit. When that day comes, you'll have the precise geometry and spec of your old machine. Just dial up those old numbers and voilà: Your love is rekindled.

If you're new to the sport or have never felt comfortable on your bike, take the time to go to the shop in your area with the best reputation for professional bike fitting. Like finding the right tailor, being positioned by a professional will make you more comfortable and save you the cost (and embarrassment) of buying a bike that doesn't fit.

FRAMESET

FRAME _____

FORK _____

SEAT TUBE _____ TOP TUBE _____

SEAT ANGLE _____ HEAD ANGLE _____

FORK RAKE _____ CHAINSTAYS _____

FRONT CENTER MEASUREMENT (FROM BOTTOM BRACKET TO FRONT AXLE) _____

BOTTOM BRACKET HEIGHT (FROM GROUND TO THE CENTER OF THE BOTTOM BRACKET) _____

COMPONENTS

SEAT _____

SEATPOST _____

STEM LENGTH _____ CM _____

HANDLEBAR _____ WIDTH _____ CM _____

HEADSET _____

SHIFTERS _____

BRAKE LEVERS _____

BRAKE CALIPERS _____

FRONT DERAILLEUR _____

REAR DERAILLEUR _____

CHAIN _____

CASSETTE _____ TEETH _____

CRANK _____ LENGTH _____ MM _____ TEETH _____

BOTTOM BRACKET _____

HUBS _____

RIMS _____

TIRES _____

TUBES _____

ACCESSORIES (BOTTLE CAGES, COMPUTER, ETC.)

_____

_____

NUTRITION

No matter how light and fast you'd like to be on your bike, you'll still need plenty of food to keep your legs strong and power your rides. Food is fuel, and without enough, your body won't charge that hill, break out in a straightaway, or throw down the hammer on the final sprint.

That said, every extra pound you carry above your ideal weight makes you 15 to 20 seconds slower for each mile of a climb. So if you're looking to drop a little drag, a balanced diet can be your closest ally.

Having a focused plan is the key to maintaining good nutrition and preventing postride binges without neglecting your calorie needs. Here are four strategies that can help you fuel up while keeping the weight off.

- **Eat breakfast:** It keeps your energy level steady so you don't overeat later in the day.
- **Weigh in:** The vast majority of people who stay slim step on a scale at least once a week—those concrete numbers staring up at you are simply too hard to ignore.
- **Be consistent:** Most folks who keep the pounds off do so by staying the course. They eat well most of the time without swinging between deprivation and bingeing.
- **Reward yourself:** Giving yourself strategic incentives (a new jersey or gloves, for example, rather than, say, cake) for healthy behavior prevents backsliding.

Follow this easy "Go Faster" formula for selecting the top cycling superfoods.

Greek yogurt (provides protein for muscle repair; calcium for fat-burning)

Oatmeal and other fiber-rich whole grains (deliver long-lasting muscle fuel)

Fresh fruits, including apples, oranges, bananas, and berries (loaded with antioxidants for muscle function and repair)

Almonds and other nuts (offer healthy fat for energy and immunity)

Spinach, carrots, broccoli, beans, and other fresh vegetables (provide vitamins and minerals for optimum muscle health)

Turkey, chicken, salmon, tofu, eggs, and other lean protein (help you feel full for longer)

Electrolyte drinks (essential for hydration during workouts)

Raisins, dates, and other dried fruits (packed with antioxidants and fiber)

Injury Fighters: Foods That Heal

When an injury takes you off the bike for a few weeks or months, your first instinct is probably to cut back on calories until it's safe to return to the saddle. But your body needs fuel to mend muscles, repair fractures, and start the road to recovery.

Get proactive about your healing process, and fight injury frustration and helplessness with proteins, vitamins, minerals, and antioxidants. Here's what to pack for your journey back to health.

PRODUCE: Carrots, spinach, sweet potatoes, and kale for vitamin A; oranges, strawberries, peppers, and broccoli for vitamin C
WHY: Vitamin A helps make white blood cells for fighting infection, and vitamin C has been proven to help skin and flesh wounds heal faster and stronger, making it a valuable ally when caring for road rash. Vitamin C also helps repair connective tissues and cartilage by contributing to the formation of collagen, an important protein that builds scar tissue, blood vessels, and even new bone cells.

MEAT: Lean turkey, sirloin, fish, and chicken
WHY: Lean meats are packed with protein, a critical building block for producing new cells and repairing damaged tissues. Because athletes require about 112 grams of protein per day (for a 175-pound male or female) for optimum healing, eating meat is an easy way to rocket toward this goal faster.

DAIRY: Eggs, milk, and yogurt
WHY: All three are good sources of protein; milk and yogurt also contain calcium, which repairs bone and muscle. The vitamin D in dairy products improves calcium absorption and helps injured muscle and bone heal.

CEREAL: Fortified cereal
WHY: It contains zinc, a proven asset to the immune system and to healing wounds. Along with red meat, fortified cereals are the best sources (some deliver 100 percent of your recommended daily value).

SEAFOOD: Salmon, tuna, and trout
WHY: In addition to an added protein bonus, fish is packed with omega-3s, fatty acids that quench the inflammation that slows recovery from tendinitis, bone fractures, and sprained ligaments.

A PERFECT DAY FOR GO FASTER MEALS

No matter what you decide is your ideal cycling weight, this go faster eating plan will help you reduce and maintain your weight. The program is based on 2,000 to 2,200 calories a day—an amount that, when combined with a metabolism-boosting riding regimen, will yield steady weight loss for most active cyclists. You'll dig into 500-calorie breakfasts, lunches, and dinners while stoking your engine between meals with energizing 250-calorie snacks. What's more, it's designed to let you mix and match your meals and snacks so you'll never be tempted to cheat.

PRE-RIDE
1 banana drizzled with honey

ON THE BIKE
1 serving of an electrolyte sports drink

1 banana

2 Fig Newton squares

BREAKFAST
Oatmeal with almond butter and fruit

A.M. SNACK
Hummus and fresh vegetables

LUNCH
Grilled chicken sandwich on whole grain bread

DINNER
Grilled turkey burger with oven-baked fries and steamed spinach

P.M. SNACK
1 apple, 1 orange, and 15 almonds

CAFFEINE ALERT

There's a lot to know about this popular pick-me-up. Consider these six stimulating truths, for example.

The Jolt Is Legit

The performance boost you get from caffeine is a result of how it hot-wires your central nervous system, says Matthew Ganio, PhD, an exercise physiologist at the Institute for Exercise and Environmental Medicine in Dallas.

"Caffeine crowds out a calming brain chemical called adenosine," he says. You become more alert, you react faster, and you don't feel like you're working as hard, all of which add up to training or competing at a higher intensity for a longer period of time and being more agile in a pack.

It Will Not Dehydrate You

"In reasonable doses, caffeine alone won't lead to more bathroom breaks during a ride or a greater risk of dehydration," says Mindy Millard-Stafford, PhD, former president of the American College of Sports Medicine. The upshot, she says, is that regardless of whether you supplement with caffeine, you don't need additional fluid to avoid performance-sapping dehydration during a ride. The long-held belief that caffeine can muck with your body's ability to regulate heat during exercise in hot weather has also been muted by science.

It Affects Everyone Differently

Before breaking out a venti on event day, Ganio suggests testing what caffeine does to you during hard training sessions. If you feel jittery, anxious, or notice your heart racing, dial back the amount you take in before a ride, says Ganio. If you can't find a caffeine level that leaves you feeling comfortable, skip it. Side effects can impair performance.

You Can Develop a Tolerance

Your body eventually adapts to the effects of caffeine, limiting the performance benefit. If you regularly drink more than five daily cups of coffee, Ganio recommends tapering your intake by a half cup a day for several days prior to a big ride, saving higher amounts of caffeine for before and during actual events.

Timing Is Everything

It takes 60 minutes for caffeine to affect the body, so imbibe 1 hour before a ride. "For rides lasting 2 hours or more, take half of your caffeine before and the other half in divided amounts during the ride," says Ganio, "making sure to consume the remainder when there is more than an hour left in your ride." Say you plan to take 200mg of caffeine for a 3-hour ride: Aim for 100mg 1 hour before you get on the bike, and 50mg at the start of each hour after.

Training Trumps It

"While caffeine can boost performance by 3 to 5 percent, training can bring about improvements by upwards of 50 percent," Ganio says. There's also the possibility of getting over-amped and going out too hard too soon, leaving you with nothing in the tank well before the ride's end. The bottom line: No amount of caffeine will turn a donkey into a thoroughbred.

DIY POST-RIDE PERK

Australian researchers found that when cyclists refueled with carbohydrates and caffeine after a ride, they accumulated 66 percent more muscle glycogen (the main fuel for working muscles) than when they ate only carbs. This DIY energy bar provides an ideal combination of the two.

INGREDIENTS

- 2 teaspoons instant espresso powder
- 1½ cup dates, chopped
- 1 cup dried figs, chopped
- ¾ cup pecans or walnuts
- ⅓ cup hempseeds
- 2 tablespoons cocoa powder
- ½ teaspoon cinnamon
- 1 tablespoon orange zest
- 1 teaspoon vanilla or coffee extract

In a bowl, dissolve espresso powder in ⅓ cup boiling water; set aside and let cool. In a food processor, pulverize dates, figs, nuts, and hempseeds. Add espresso, cocoa, cinnamon, orange zest, and extract; process until clumps form. Place mixture on a lightly greased baking sheet and form into a ½-inch-thick square. Freeze for 30 minutes, then slice into 10 bars.

PER BAR: 177 calories, 7g fat, 30g carbohydrates, 5g fiber, 5g protein, 15mg caffeine

LATHER UP!

Help prevent cancer—and freaky tan lines—by using sunscreen on every ride. Here's how to defend yourself.

Three-Step Protection

1. Apply at least one ounce, or an espresso-shot worth, of sunscreen 30 minutes before your ride so your skin has time to absorb it.

2. Make sure it gets under the edges of your clothing, which can shift as you ride and expose the skin underneath—or apply it before you kit up.

3. Reapply every 2 hours (sooner if you're sweating profusely).

Kathleen Welsh, MD, a dermatologist in San Francisco, recommends choosing a formula with an SPF of 30 or higher that protects against UVA and UVB rays (or says "broad-spectrum" on the label). Chemical blocks (such as avobenzone or oxybenzone) absorb UV rays before they harm you; physical blocks (titanium dioxide or zinc oxide) reflect sunlight. Wear sunscreen even on overcast days: 80 percent of UV rays penetrate cloud cover.

GEAR GUIDE
15 Tools You Should Own

A flat tire. A loose bolt. You'll want to have tools on hand for day-to-day maintenance, but setting up a home shop requires garage space and money for expensive hardware. That's why we've condensed the workshops and tool kits of pro mechanics down to 15 essentials. Don't drag your bike to the shop for every basic repair: Stock these trusty tools for your own DIY repairs.

1. Chain Checker: Chains and cogsets are becoming increasingly expensive, but Park Tool's CC-2 will accurately gauge your chain's life in real terms, so you don't toss one that still has miles to go—and you don't keep using one so worn that it starts eating your cassette cogs alive.

2. Torx Keys: Disc-brake-rotor hardware is nearly all Torx already, and Campagnolo uses Torx on many of its newest components, as does SRAM throughout its XX group and FSA for chainring bolts. Three sizes will cover everything

you need: T-10, T-25, and T-30. Park Tool makes a folding set that has these sizes and more.

3. Floor Pump: The question is: Which one to get? There are plenty of serviceable models, but after consulting with pro mechanics, we recommend an SKS Airbase Pro pump.

4. Minipump: The Crank Brothers Power Pump Alloy has a durable, CNC-machined barrel and accurate dial gauge. Set it to high volume to fill tires quickly to about 80 psi; when the pumping gets tough, twist a knob to switch into high pressure mode and inflate up to 130 psi.

5. Chain Tool: These come in many varieties, but for a 10-speed drivetrain, the Shimano TL-CN32 might be the finest tool on the market. And your 11-speed drivetrain calls for the precision and function of Campagnolo's UN-CT300.

6. 8-, 9-, and 10mm Combination Wrenches: Tighten the small nuts and hex bolts on accessories like racks and fenders. Snap-On wrenches are legendary for their quality and inexpensive at such teeny sizes.

7. Tire Levers: If you have Mavic wheels, it's best to change tires with Mavic levers. Even if you don't, the broad, flat blade and rigid plastic build make them kind to tires and rims and just as effective on stubborn ones.

8. Cable Cutter: The Felco C-7 cutter has been known to last more than 20 years, justifying its expensive cost. You just can't argue with longevity like that.

9. Compact Scissors: Many pros choose Fiskars 5-inch Micro-Tip scissors. They're handy for trimming handlebar wrap and snipping vinyl tape.

10. Hex Keys: Also referred to by the brand name Allen, these are probably the most obvious hand tool necessity for every cyclist. Bondhus is a popular brand, known for its often-copied ball-shaped tip, which allows you to easily spin bolts from angles where access is limited. Get the following sizes: 1.5-, 2-, 2.5-, 3-, 4-, 5-, 6-, 8-, and 10mm.

11. Vise-Whip and Cassette Lockring Tool with Guide Pins and Handle: When it's time to change your cogset, Pedro's cool, high-tech Vise-Whip locks into place on your cog, eliminating the chances of a knuckle-busting slip. Pair it with the Cyclus cassette lockring tool that has both Shimano/SRAM and Campagnolo lockring compatibility built into a single two-sided tool.

12. Multitool: Always carry a palm-size workshop like the Lezyne RAP 13, which boasts eight sizes of hex and Torx keys, a Phillips screwdriver, a chain tool, two sizes of standard square spoke wrenches, and a third spoke wrench for Mavic splined nipples.

13. Four-Way Screwdriver: Those who appreciate space efficiency and multitasking will dig this tool. Choose a version with quality steel tips that won't round off or strip hardware. The four sizes will fit nearly every flat or Phillips screw on your bike.

14. Spoke Wrenches: With so many wheel manufacturers using unique spoke-nipple designs, it's impossible to recommend any one model. If you have conventional square spoke nipples on your wheels, you can't go wrong with Park Tool's SW-0, SW-1, or SW-2.

15. Sharpened Spoke: A sharp pick has many uses, from opening the liner on a freshly cut piece of cable housing to poking leaves out of a cogset. You can sharpen the end of a broken spoke with a hand file to make your own. Bend a loop at the other end so you can hang it on a Peg-Board.

EQUIPMENT LOGS

Gear I used this year and why.

You pop into a bike shop for a tube and a couple of energy bars and walk out $9 lighter. No big deal, right? What if we told you that the average enthusiast spends nearly $3,000 on inner tubes alone over a lifetime of cycling? What if we told you that same person spends $11,000 on energy food? What if we gave you the grand total: a whopping $121,253 spent on equipment over the average cyclist's life on two wheels?

You'd probably want to find a way to keep track of your purchases. We've provided the spaces below for that reason. As with the rest of this training journal, be sure to include as much information as possible—you never know which mundane detail might save you thousands of dollars in the long run.

ITEM: _____

DATE PURCHASED _____

PURCHASED FROM _____

PRICE PAID _____ SIZE _____

FEATURES _____

OVERALL IMPRESSION _____

WOULD YOU PURCHASE THIS AGAIN? _____

ITEM: _____

DATE PURCHASED _____

PURCHASED FROM _____

PRICE PAID _____ SIZE _____

FEATURES _____

OVERALL IMPRESSION _____

WOULD YOU PURCHASE THIS AGAIN? _____

ITEM: _____

DATE PURCHASED _____

PURCHASED FROM _____

PRICE PAID _____ SIZE _____

FEATURES _____

OVERALL IMPRESSION _____

WOULD YOU PURCHASE THIS AGAIN? _____

ITEM: _____

DATE PURCHASED _____

PURCHASED FROM _____

PRICE PAID _____ SIZE _____

FEATURES _____

OVERALL IMPRESSION _____

WOULD YOU PURCHASE THIS AGAIN? _____

ITEM: _____

DATE PURCHASED _____

PURCHASED FROM _____

PRICE PAID _____ SIZE _____

FEATURES _____

OVERALL IMPRESSION _____

WOULD YOU PURCHASE THIS AGAIN? _____

ITEM: _____

DATE PURCHASED _____

PURCHASED FROM _____

PRICE PAID _____ SIZE _____

FEATURES _____

OVERALL IMPRESSION _____

WOULD YOU PURCHASE THIS AGAIN? _____

ITEM: _____

DATE PURCHASED _____

PURCHASED FROM _____

PRICE PAID _____ SIZE _____

FEATURES _____

OVERALL IMPRESSION _____

WOULD YOU PURCHASE THIS AGAIN? _____

ITEM: _____

DATE PURCHASED _____

PURCHASED FROM _____

PRICE PAID _____ SIZE _____

FEATURES _____

OVERALL IMPRESSION _____

WOULD YOU PURCHASE THIS AGAIN? _____

ITEM: _____

DATE PURCHASED _____

PURCHASED FROM _____

PRICE PAID _____ SIZE _____

FEATURES _____

OVERALL IMPRESSION _____

WOULD YOU PURCHASE THIS AGAIN? _____

ITEM: _____

DATE PURCHASED _____

PURCHASED FROM _____

PRICE PAID _____ SIZE _____

FEATURES _____

OVERALL IMPRESSION _____

WOULD YOU PURCHASE THIS AGAIN? _____

FIX IT OR NIX IT?

Use this handy guide to figure out whether your gear can be saved, or if it needs to be replaced.

FRAME

REPAIR If money's no object, or you spent too much on your frame to just trash it. Any frame can be fixed, even carbon (go to bicycling.com/resurrection).

REPLACE If you've been lusting for a new bike and need an excuse to get one.

YOU'RE PUSHIN' IT If you ride it after a wreck without inspecting for damage. Look for cracks, bends, and paint bulges.

CHAIN

REPAIR If the length of 24 links, rivet to rivet, doesn't exceed $12\frac{1}{16}$ inches. Or, the chain has seen less than a season.

REPLACE When it exceeds the $\frac{1}{16}$-inch cutoff. Pins and rollers are worn, making the holes in the sideplates oval.

YOU'RE PUSHIN' IT If it's your third season on a repaired chain. You may damage your cassette and chainrings.

CLEATS

REPAIR When it's hard to get in and out of pedals. If your cleats aren't worn or broken, tighten the bolts.

REPLACE If you twist excessively to unclip or can't stay clipped in; pedals don't feel secure to the cleat.

YOU'RE PUSHIN' IT If you're missing a cleat bolt. The cleat could shift position and cause you to crash.

HELMET

REPAIR When the visor is damaged, pads are missing, or the fastener is broken.

REPLACE If you've taken a hard fall, it's cracked, or you don't remember when you bought it.

YOU'RE PUSHIN' IT If you often store it in direct sunlight—UV rays break down the helmet's protective materials.

PEDALS

REPAIR If you hear a click with each pedal stroke. The pedal may have loosened.

REPLACE Your pedal wobbles when you ride. You probably bent the spindle. Replace it or get new pedals.

YOU'RE PUSHIN' IT If you ride on a wobbly pedal for so long, you develop ankle or knee problems.

RIM

REPAIR If a wheel develops a minor wobble; check for broken spokes.

REPLACE If the brake track is concave; you see cracks around spoke eyelets.

YOU'RE PUSHIN' IT If your brake pads hit your rim, so you adjust them to sit wider.

SADDLE

REPAIR If there's a tear in an unobtrusive place; rails seem unaffected.

REPLACE If something's poking you; rails feel loose or are bent.

YOU'RE PUSHIN' IT If the saddle is smashed down to the top of the seatpost.

SHIFT/BRAKE CABLES

REPAIR If shifting is sluggish but cables are rust-free. Drip a light lube into the housing.

REPLACE If cables are rusted, ends are frayed, or wires poke out.

YOU'RE PUSHIN' IT If you snip the rusty frayed ends and keep riding.

SHIFT/BRAKE LEVER

REPAIR If it's turned (not bent). Push it into position and look for visible damage.

REPLACE When the shifter is cracked and/or the lever is bent or in pieces.

YOU'RE PUSHIN' IT If you hear a cracking noise beneath your hands and keep riding anyway.

TIRE

REPAIR When the cut can be patched (try Park Tool's TB-2 Emergency Tire Boot), or the tread area hasn't flattened.

REPLACE If the hole is larger than 1 inch, or you see beads or bulges.

YOU'RE PUSHIN' IT If you can flake bits of rubber off the tread.

TUBE

REPAIR If your flat was caused by a puncture or pinch.

REPLACE When the hole or leak is at the base of the valve stem—a patch can't fix this.

YOU'RE PUSHIN' IT There's no pushing it. You can either fix it or you can't.

BIKE MAINTENANCE
Simple Repairs You Can Master

REAR DERAILLEUR

Clunky rear shifting is most often caused when the cable stretches or the amount of tension it exerts on the derailleur somehow goes out of whack, which affects the derailleur's alignment with the cogs. But don't fiddle with the limit screws: The simplest way to tune the rear shifting solves around 90 percent of all problems. Shift to the smallest cog. Turning one pedal by hand, click up one gear. If the derailleur balks, click back and stop the drivetrain. Turn the barrel adjuster—located where the cable goes into the derailleur—out half a turn (counterclockwise). Try the shift again, continuing to dial out the adjuster as needed until the derailleur snaps crisply onto the cog. Progress up the cogs. When the shifting is perfect that way, repeat the routine coming down the cogset. This time if the derailleur hesitates, dial the barrel adjuster in just one-quarter of a turn at a time. You should be able to work your way up and down the cogset and fine-tune the shifting in less than 10 minutes.

CHAIN

CLEAN: Soap up a sponge (or use commercial degreaser or cleanser), and wrap the sponge around the chain and under the chainstay. Use your other hand to backpedal 10 revolutions so that the chain is pulled through the sponge. Rinse the sponge, squeeze out excess water, reload with cleaner, and repeat. Continue this process until the sponge no longer gets dirty. To dry, backpedal the chain through a clean rag, or let it sit for 10 minutes. Apply one drop of lube to each of the chain's pins, then backpedal 10 revolutions, allow 5 minutes for the lube to penetrate, and then wipe the chain with a clean rag by backpedaling. Your chain will stay in top shape if you repeat this process every 2 weeks or immediately after wet rides. **CHECK FOR WEAR:** You'll hear chain wear called stretching, but the plates don't actually get longer—the pins that hold the links together degrade, creating slack so that the chain doesn't sit properly on the teeth of the cassette or chainrings. You can detect wear with a special tool, but here's the simplest method: With the chain on the small ring, apply force to the right pedal with one hand while holding the rear wheel stationary with the other. If the chain floats above the teeth rather than fully meshing with them, it's time for a new one. Take this measurement every 500 miles.

BOTTOM BRACKET/CRANKSET

With the chain derailed, spin the crankset slowly with one finger. If the movement feels gritty, audibly grinds, or catches at certain spots in the rotation, you need either a bottom bracket overhaul or full replacement. Take your bike into a shop.

1. Grab the crankarms and try to wiggle them toward and away from the frame. If there is play, determine if the whole crankset is moving or if it's only one of the crankarms.

2. For the crankarm, try tightening with an 8mm hex, a thin-walled socket, or a proprietary tool and then check again. For the crankset itself, a shop might be able to tighten the BB or else replace it.

3. Snug all chainring bolts, usually with a 5mm hex or a Torx key. And from now on, check it once a month.

CABLES AND HOUSING

If shifting or braking feels sluggish, the problem is often solved with a simple cleaning of gummed-up housings or dirty cables. Create slack in the brake cables by opening the quick-release buttons (on the calipers for Shimano and SRAM, on the lever for Campagnolo). To slacken the rear derailleur cable: Shift to the largest cog while turning the pedals; stop the pedals

and rear wheel, then push the shifter as if to return to the smallest cog; because the derailleur won't move, the cable slackens. With the tension gone, you can easily slip the housings out of the stops, then slide them along the cables to expose dirt and grit. Wipe the newly exposed sections of the cables clean, then spray degreaser into one end of each housing until it drips cleanly out of the other end. Most modern cables don't need lube for smooth operation, but you might want to try it to see if friction is reduced; place a drop or two of lube on your thumb and forefinger, then pinch the cable between them and wipe any exposable sections. Replace the housings in the stops, tighten the quick releases, and gently pedal the rear derailleur into the proper gear. If the shifting is still sluggish or the cables appeared frayed, rusted, or bent, take your bike to the shop for a replacement.

BRAKE PADS

Examine the pads and remove embedded grit or metal shards (which come from your rim) with an awl, tweezers, or other sharp implement. Then roughen the surface with sandpa-

per or a file to improve braking. Replace the set if either pad is too hard to let you press in with your thumbnail, or if the grooves etched into the pad are so worn they're almost nonexistent.

HEADSET

Left unaddressed, a loose headset could cause you to lose control, impair steering, and eventually damage your head tube and fork. With your bike in a stand or sitting on the ground, grab the handlebar with one hand and the front wheel with the other, then push and pull in opposition while feeling for play. To tighten, loosen the two bolts that clamp the stem to the steerer tube, then turn the bolt in the top cap of the stem clockwise and retighten the clamping bolts to the manufacturer's recommended torque. The headset is just right when there is no slop when you perform the check, but the front wheel freely flops from side to side when you pick up the front of the bike. You might need several attempts to find the precise adjustment. Make sure you always loosen the clamp bolts before tightening the cap.

WHEEL

TO TRUE A WHEEL: First, if your wheel is hopping, take it to a shop. If it's just wobbling slightly to one side, try spinning the wheel to locate the defiant section. On that side of the wheel, loosen the two spokes closest to the wobble one-quarter turn with a spoke wrench. On the other side of the wheel, tighten the two closest spokes one-quarter turn. (Turning the nipple clockwise tightens the spoke, counterclockwise loosens it.) Spin the wheel and tune the wobble again. Never turn the nipples more than a quarter-turn at a time, and be prepared to take your time working it back and forth, loosening or tightening several times on each side until you've restored a smooth spin to your wheel.

RIDING RESOURCES

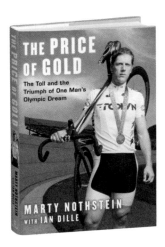

The Price of Gold
The Toll and the Triumph of One Man's Olympic Dream
by Marty Nothstein with Ian Dille

Marty Nothstein arrived at the 1996 Olympic games in Atlanta as a heavy favorite in the match sprint. But Nothstein lost the race by a hair's width on the finish line. At the medal ceremony, he vowed to come back to the Olympics in another 4 years to at last win the gold. "I didn't come here for a silver medal," he said.

In *The Price of Gold*, Nothstein eloquently and honestly tracks his journey to the Games in Sydney and the life events that molded him into the world's fastest man on a bicycle—from his tough-love upbringing to the "borderline outlaw" cast of cycling characters who helped guide him through the ranks. Nothstein's Olympic victory in 2000 would place him firmly among the world's greatest track cyclists of all time.

Sure to be a sports classic, this is the harrowing, triumphant tale of a cyclist's journey to Olympic victory and the price he paid to achieve greatness.

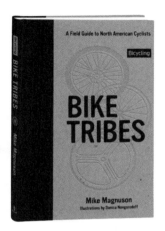

Bike Tribes
A Field Guide to North American Cyclists
by Mike Magnuson

Anyone who rides a bike knows that the bicycling world is made up of tribes. There are the spandex-clad weekend warriors, the hipsters on street bikes, the tattooed bike messengers, and that's just to name a few. They may look like they live on different planets, but they are united by their abiding love of bikes—and often by their total disdain of other members of this insular world.

Bike Tribes is a hip, illustrated guide to the many incarnations of bicyclists. It's *The Official Preppy Handbook* of bicycling, replete with one-of-a-kind illustra-tions that introduce the special habits, clothing, preferences, and predilections of cyclists.

Mike Magnuson, an avid rider, bicycling expert, and longtime contributor to *Bicycling* magazine, covers the basics of racing, etiquette, apparel, and gear, while includ-ing hilarious running commentary on cycling culture, poking holes in practically every pretension in the cycling world. *Bike Tribes* is a fun romp through the various subcultures in the bike community—bound to appeal to newcomers and griz-zled cyclists alike.

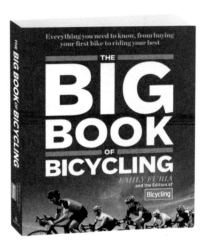

The Big Book of Bicycling

by Emily Furia and the Editors of *Bicycling*®

Cycling is experiencing an exciting boom in popularity, fueled by the growth of cause rides, triathlons, bike commuting, and more. It's a sport that lets people have fun while they get fit, and no one knows it better than the experts at *Bicycling* magazine.

Here, *Bicycling* assembles its best advice in a must-have book that cyclists of all levels can refer to again and again for answers to all of their cycling questions. Senior Editor Emily Furia and her colleagues have organized the latest, most useful information on getting started, buying a bike, riding to work, bicycle maintenance, fitness and nutrition, teaching your child to ride, understanding the rules of the road, and much, much more. Needless to say, *The Big Book of Bicycling* is an invaluable resource for cyclists of all levels.

The Bicycling® Guide to Complete Bicycle Maintenance & Repair

by Todd Downs

Whether you own the latest model or a classic with thousands of miles on it, beginner and experienced cyclists alike need a guide that will help them get their bikes out of the shop faster and keep them on the road longer. For decades, the bestselling *The Bicycling® Guide to Complete Bicycle Maintenance & Repair* from the world's leading authority on cycling has done just that.

With troubleshooting sections to quickly identify and correct common problems, 450 photographs, and 40 drawings to clarify all the step-by-step directions so even the complete neophyte can get repairs right the first time, this is truly the ultimate bicycle repair and maintenance manual. Now better than ever, the newest edition contains information on component kits and carbon fork specifications.

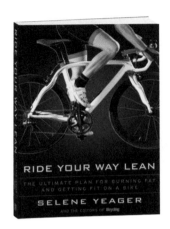

Ride Your Way Lean
The Ultimate Plan for Burning Fat and Getting Fit on a Bike

by Selene Yeager and the editors of *Bicycling*®

Forget gym memberships and long, boring hours on the cardio machine. In this book, *Bicycling* magazine columnist and resident "Fit Chick" Selene Yeager shows that by varying your rides and incorporating elements such as intervals and hill work, cycling can easily burn more than 600 calories per hour. Each chapter is seasoned with anecdotal advice, success stories, pitfalls, and other advice from real people who have lost 30, 50, or even 100 pounds through cycling. By following Yeager's training plans (created with the founder of Performance Driven Coaching, James Herrera) and her sensible nutritional advice, you can embark on a weight-loss journey that is both effective and fun.

Ride Fast
Get Up to Speed on Your Bike in 10 Weeks or Less

by Eric Harr

Whether your bicycle is already a key part of your workout routine or it is just sitting in your garage, ignored, Eric Harr has some news for you: That same cherished relic of your childhood is your ticket to better health, boundless energy, and an incredibly effective workout routine. All you have to do is get out there and get started.

In *Ride Fast*, Harr presents readers with an easy-to-follow 10-week program that helps even the most inexperienced cyclists gradually build up their speed to 25 miles per hour. Harr even shows you how to incorporate your loved ones into your workout, describing ways for the whole family to be out on the road together. Along the way you'll learn how to master the nuances of riding fast, what foods provide the most energy, and how to make time for your bike even when you're swamped. Once upon a time, you couldn't wait to pedal your 10-speed around the neighborhood, pushing it as fast as it could go. Wouldn't you like to feel that way again?

Get ready, get set, ride fast!

Bicycling Magazine's
New Cyclist Handbook

Edited by Ben Hewitt

This comprehensive handbook will help any new cyclist ride with confidence and avoid common pitfalls. Learn how to choose the right bike, ride safely in traffic, treat and prevent injuries, train for a century, and perform basic maintenance. Packed with quick tips from the pros at *Bicycling* magazine, this volume provides everything the new cyclist needs to know to achieve optimum performance cycling.

Bicycling Magazine's 1,000 All-Time Best Tips

Edited by Ben Hewitt

J ump-start your cycling savvy with this compilation of proven tips from the staff of *Bicycling* magazine. Enjoy nuggets of wisdom from experts in the full range of cycling subjects—from aerodynamics to heart rate training zones. Bursting with smart strategies to build your skill level, this is a book guaranteed to make you a more talented cyclist.

GLOSSARY

A

ADJUSTABLE CUP: the left-hand cup in a nonsealed bottom bracket, used in adjusting the bottom bracket bearings; removed during bottom bracket overhaul

AERO LEVERS: road bike brake levers employing hidden cables that travel out the back of the lever body and under the handlebar tape

ALLEN WRENCH: a specific brand of hex key

ALL-MOUNTAIN BIKE: a mountain bike designed to balance climbing and descending abilities with slightly more emphasis on descending prowess; features dual-suspension with 4 to 6 inches of travel

ALL-TERRAIN BIKE (ATB): a term sometimes used for mountain bike

AXLE: a stationary rod around which a body rotates, such as a hub axle

B

BAR-ENDS: short, forward-reaching extensions that fit on the ends of a mountain bike handlebar to add another riding position

B/B OR BB: common shorthand for bottom bracket

BINDER BOLT: the bolt used to fasten a stem inside a steerer tube, a seatpost inside a seat tube, or a handlebar or fork steerer in a stem

BMX (BICYCLE MOTO CROSS): a type of racing done on a closed dirt track over obstacles, usually on 20- or 24-inch wheel bikes with one gear

BOTTOM BRACKET: the cylindrical part of a bicycle frame that holds the crankset axle, two sets of ball bearings, a fixed cup, and an adjustable cup

BRAKE PAD: (1) a block of hard rubber, urethane, or cork material fastened to the end of a rim-brake caliper; it presses against the wheel rim when the brakes are applied, also known as a brake block; (2) a thin block of resin, organix, or metallic-compound material that is clamped onto the disc (of a disc brake system) by the caliper

BRAKE SHOE: the metal part that holds a brake pad and is bolted to the end of a brake caliper

BRAZE-ONS: parts for mounting shift levers, derailleurs, water bottle cages, and racks, which are fastened to a bicycle frame through a type of soldering process known as brazing

BRINELLING: a type of wear in bearing components characterized by a series of dents in the races or cups

BUTTED TUBING: L tubing of carried diameter or wall thickness, used to maintain or increase strength at the ends while reducing weight in the middle, where less strength is required

C

CABLE CAP: a small aluminum cap installed on the ends of brake and shift cables to keep them from fraying; also known as a cable crimp

CALIPERS: (1) brake arms that reach around the sides of a wheel to press brake pads against the wheel rim; (2) the fixed portion of a disc brake system that houses the pistons and brake pads

CANTILEVER BRAKES: rim brakes with pivoting arms mounted on fork blades or seatstays

CASSETTE: a cluster of rear cogs that fits onto a cassette hub

CASSETTE HUB: a type of rear hub that has a built-in freewheel mechanism

CHAIN: the series of links pinned together that extends from the chainring to the cogs on the back wheel and allows you to propel the bike by pedaling

CHAINRING (OR CHAINWHEEL): a sprocket attached to the right crankarm to drive the chain

CHAINRING NUT SPANNER: a special tool used to loosen the slotted chainring bolts (the ones behind the inner ring) that fasten a chainring to a crankarm

CHAINSTAYS: the two tubes of a bicycle frame that run from the bottom bracket to the rear dropouts

CHAIN WHIP: a tool consisting of a metal bar and two sections of chain, used to hold a cassette steady while the lockring is removed

CIRCUIT: a road cycling race course in the form of a loop

CIRCUIT RACE: a road race that takes place on a long circuit as defined by the UCI and USA Cycling, measuring at least 8 kilometers (5 miles) per lap

CLIPLESS PEDALS: pedals that use a releasable mechanism like that of a ski binding to lock onto cleated shoes; these pedals do not use toeclips or toe straps

COASTER BRAKE: a foot-operated brake built into the rear hub; normally found on one-speed kids' bikes and cruisers

COG: a sprocket that is attached directly to the rear hub on a single-speed bike or mounted as part of a cassette on a multispeed bike

COGSET: a cluster of sprockets that fit onto a cassette hub or freewheel body

CONE: a bearing race that curves to the inside of a circle of ball bearings and works in conjunction with a cup

COTTERED CRANKSET: a crankset in which the crankarms are fastened to the axle by means of threaded cotters and nuts

COTTERLESS CRANKSET: a crankset in which the crankarms are fastened to the axle by means of a precision-fit taper and nuts or bolts (instead of cotters)

CRANKARM: a part, one end of which is attached to the bottom bracket axle and the other of which holds a pedal that, through its forward rotation, provides the leverage needed to power the bicycle

CRANKARM BOLT: the bolt that holds the crankarm onto the end of the axle in a cotterless crankset

CRITERIUM: a form of road cycling competition that takes place on a short circuit, measured in time (from 30 to 90 minutes) or distance (19 to 62 miles)

CROSS-COUNTRY BIKE: a mountain bike suited to racing or general off-road riding on varied terrain

CROSS-COUNTRY RACE: a form of mountain bike competition that takes place on an off-road circuit that may be comprised of forest roads, forest or field trails, unpaved dirt or gravel roads, or any combination of these

CROSSOVER CABLE: see Straddle cable

C-SPANNER: a wrench with a C-shaped end that is used to loosen the lockring on certain bottom brackets and headsets

CYCLOCROSS BIKE: a bicycle designed specifically for cyclocross racing; features include specific geometry, drop handlebars, knobby tires, and cantilever brakes

D

DERAILLEUR: a mechanism mounted to the seat tube or derailleur hanger of a frame that pushes the chain off one sprocket and onto another

DERAILLEUR HANGER: a threaded metal piece that extends below the right rear dropout and is used as a mount for the rear derailleur

DIAMOND FRAME: the traditional bicycle frame, the principal parts of which form a diamond shape

DISC BRAKE: a braking system that uses a small caliper mounted near a front or rear dropout that clamps onto a stainless steel disc attached to the hub to generate braking force

DOWNHILL BIKE: a bike designed for racing down mountains; features include long-travel (7 inches or more) dual-suspension frame, powerful disc brakes with 7- or 8-inch diameter discs, and in many cases a single chainring with special chain guides and retention systems

DOWNHILL RACE: a mountain bike time trial that takes place on a steeply descending course comprised of trail and/or dirt or gravel road, sometimes with jumps, drops, or other technical trail features

DOWN TUBE: the frame tube running from the headset to the bottom bracket; one part of the main triangle on a bicycle frame

DRAFTING: tucking in closely behind another rider so he or she will break the wind, saving you energy

DRIVETRAIN: the derailleurs, chain, cogset, and crankset of a bike

DROP: (1) the vertical distance from the horizontal line connecting the two wheel axles to the horizontal centerline of the bottom bracket; one way of determining the location of the bottom bracket in relation to the rest of the bicycle frame; (2) the vertical distance from a horizontal line across the top of the saddle to the horizontal centerline of the handlebar; one of the measurements of bike fit

DROPOUT: slots in the frame and fork into which the rear and front wheel axles fit

DROPS: the curved portions below the brake lever bodies of a road-type handlebar

DUAL SLALOM: a mountain bike competition in which two riders race down similar but separate downhill courses, sometimes with banked turns, jumps, and other technical features

DUAL-SUSPENSION BIKE: a bike with front and rear suspension; casually referred to as a "dualie" or "fully"

DUSTCAP: a metal or plastic cap that fits into a hub shell to keep contaminant out of hub bearings; or a metal or plastic end cover to prevent contamination of the bearings on the outside face of a pedal or for the fixing bolt of a crankarm

E

END PLUGS: the caps that fit onto or into the ends of the handlebars

F

FACE: to shave the outer edges of a bottom bracket shell or the upper and lower ends of a head tube to make them parallel with one another and square to the tube's centerline so that, when the bottom bracket or headset is installed, the bearings will run as smoothly as possible

FERRULES: removable cylindrical metal or plastic caps used to reinforce the ends of cable housing

FIXED CUP: the right-hand cup in a loose-ball bottom bracket

FIXED GEAR (WHEEL): as found on track-racing and some urban transportation bikes, a hub-and-cog combination that's designed in such a way that one must always pedal; it's impossible to coast

FIXING BOLT: a bolt used to hold a crankarm on the spindle of a crankset

FLANGE: the part of a hub shell to which spokes are attached

FORK: the part of the frame that fits inside the head tube and holds the front wheel; a term also sometimes applied to the part of the frame where chainstays and seatstays join to hold the rear axle

FORK BLADES: the tubes of a fork that extend down from the crown and end with the dropouts that hold the front wheel

FORK CROWN: the point where the fork blades are joined with the steerer tube

FORK RAKE: the shortest distance between the front axle and an imaginary line extending through the head tube down toward the ground

FORK TIPS: the slotted tips of the fork blades into which the front wheel axle fits; also called dropouts

FOUR CROSS (4X): see Mountain cross

FREERIDE BIKE: a type of mountain bike designed to ride the most technical and punishing or downhill trails; features include long-travel dual-suspension and components manufactured for ultimate strength

FREEWHEEL: a removable component on the rear hub that carries gear cogs on the outside and contains a ratcheting mechanism inside that provides the connection to the wheel for pedaling while also allowing coasting; sometimes used to refer to the ratcheting mechanism inside a cassette

FRICTION SHIFTERS: conventional (nonindex) levers that retain their position through the use of friction washers

FRONT TRIANGLE: not really a triangle but a quadrilateral with one short side, it is the section of a bicycle frame that consists of the head tube, top tube, seat tube, and down tube

G

GEAR: one position on a drivetrain; for example, being on the largest chainring and smallest rear cog is the largest gear

GRIPS: the rubber or foam sleeves that fit on the ends of upright handlebars; you grip them when riding

H

HEADSET: the combination of cups, cones, and ball bearings that creates the bearing mechanism that allows the fork column to rotate inside the head tube so you can steer

HEAD TUBE: the shortest tube in the main triangle; the one in which the fork's steerer tube rotates

HEX KEY: a small, often L-shaped hexagonal wrench that fits inside the head of a bolt or screw; sometimes referred to as an Allen key or Allen wrench

HOUSING: the plastic-covered tubing inside which cables run

HUB: the center of a wheel, consisting of a shell to which spokes attach and containing an axle along with two sets of bearings, bearing cones, lockwashers, locknuts, and parts for attaching the wheel to the frame

HUB BRAKE: any type of brake (disc, drum, or coaster) that operates through the wheel hub rather than the rim

HYDRAULIC BRAKE: a brake relying on a sealed fluid system instead of a cable for operation

I

IDLER PULLEY: the pulley in a rear derailleur that stays farthest from the cassette cogs and keeps tension on the chain; sometimes called the tension pulley

IMBA (INTERNATIONAL MOUNTAIN BICYCLING ASSOCIATION): an organization that protects mountain bike trails

INDEX SHIFTERS: levers that "click" into distinct positions that correspond to certain cassette cogs and don't require fine-tuning after each shift

J

JOCKEY PULLEY: the pulley in a rear derailleur that stays closest to the cogs and guides the chain from cog to cog during a gear shift; sometimes called the guide pulley

K

KNOBBY TIRES: heavy-duty tires with large rubber knobs spaced relatively far apart to provide traction on off-road terrain

L

LEFT-HAND THREADING: threading that's the opposite of regular threading, meaning you must turn left to tighten and right to loosen; always found on the left pedal; also known as reverse threading

LINKING CABLE: see Straddle cable

LOADED TOURER: a bicycle with structural strength, geometry, and equipment that is designed to allow a cyclist to travel with a full load of gear

LOCKNUT: a nut on a hub axle that is tightened against an axle cone to maintain the bearing adjustment; the locknut is also a hub's point of contact with the inside surface of a dropout

LOCKRING: (1) the notched ring that fits on the left side of some bottom brackets and prevents the adjustable cup from turning; (2) the left-hand-threaded, notched ring that prevents the cog from coming loose on a fixed gear wheel

LOCKWASHER: a washer with a small metal tab to prevent it from turning, such as the washer beneath the locknut on a threaded headset or between the locknut and cone on some older hubs

LOOSE BALL BEARINGS: bearings inside a component that are not held in a metal or plastic retainer

LUG: an external metal sleeve that holds two or more tubes together at the joints of a frame

M

MAIN TRIANGLE: see Front triangle

MARATHON: a long-distance cross-country mountain bike race; typically ranges in length between 60 and 100 kilometers (37 and 62 miles)

MARATHON BIKE: a mountain bike for cross-country endurance races generally light-weight and often with around 4 inches of suspension travel to balance performance and long-ride comfort

MIXTE FRAME: a frame that replaces the top tube with twin lateral tubes that run all the way from the head tube back to the rear dropouts

MOUNTAIN BIKE: a bicycle with an upright handlebar, sturdy fat tires, and wide-range gearing designed for off-road use

MOUNTAIN CROSS: a mountain bike competition in which four riders at a time race down a prepared downhill track with banked turns, jumps, and other technical features; also called four cross

N

NIPPLE: a small metal piece that fits through a wheel rim and is threaded inside to receive the end of a spoke

P

PANNIERS: luggage bags used in pairs and fastened alongside one or both wheels of a bike

PIN SPANNER: a wrench with pins on forked ends that is used to turn certain adjustable cups on some bottomless brackets

PLAIN-GAUGE TUBING: tubing whose thickness and diameter remain constant over its entire length; aka straight-gauge tubing

PRELOAD: an important suspension adjustment that usually involves modifying air pressure or adjusting the spring to ensure that the suspension responds appropriately to the rider's weight

Q

QUICK LINK: a special connecting link that allows derailleur-type chains to be disassembled and reassembled without the use of tools

QUICK RELEASE: a cam-lever mechanism used to rapidly tighten or loosen a wheel on a bike frame or a seatpost in a seat tube

QUICK-RELEASE SKEWER: a thin rod that runs through the center of a wheel axle; a cam lever is attached to one end, and the other end is threaded to receive a nut

QUILL: the part of a stem that fits inside the fork's steerer tube; quilled stems are used with threaded-type forks and headsets

R

RACES: curved metal surfaces of cups and cones that ball bearings contact as they roll

REAR TRIANGLE: a frame triangle formed by the chainstays, seatstays, and seat tube

RECUMBENT: a bike that places the rider in a reclining feet-first position

REGULAR THREADING: the threading that's found on almost all bike parts; turn to the right to tighten and to the left to loosen

RETAINER: a metal or plastic ring that holds the bearings in place in a headset or bottom bracket

REVERSE THREADING: see Left-hand threading

RIM: the metal hoop of a wheel that holds the tire, tube, and outer ends of the spokes

RIM BRAKE: any type of brake that slows or stops a wheel by pressing its pads against the sides of the wheel rim

RISER BAR: a mountain bike handlebar that sweeps upward so the ends (where the grips fit) are higher than the center (where the stem clamps)

ROAD BIKE: a lightweight, multispeed bicycle characterized by a drop handlebar

ROAD RACE: a form of bicycle competition involving cyclists on road bikes; take place over a long course that typically range in length from 80 to 200 kilometers (50 to 124 miles)

ROLLERS: a stationary training device with a boxlike frame and three rotating cyclinders (one for the front wheel and two for the rear wheel) on which the bicycle is balanced and ridden

S

SADDLE: the seat on a bicycle

SEALED BEARINGS: bearings fastened in sealed containers to keep out contaminants

SEAMED TUBING: tubing made from metal strip stock that is curved until its edges meet, then welded together

SEAMLESS TUBING: tubing made from blocks of metal that are pierced and drawn into tube shape

SEAT CLUSTER: the conjunction of top tube, seat tube, and seatstays near the top of the seat tube

SEATMAST: a feature of a frame that does not use a traditional seatpost; instead, the seat tube is extended up past the top tube and is fitted with a capital that holds the saddle

SEATPOST: the part to which the saddle clamps and which fits down inside the seat tube

SEATSTAYS: parallel tubes that run from the top of the seat tube back to the rear axle

SEAT TUBE: the tube that runs from the seat cluster to the bottom bracket

SEMISLICK TIRE: a type of mountain bike tire with limited tread; popular for not-too-technical courses because it rolls faster than a knobby tire

SHALLOW ANGLES: angles that position frame tubes farther from vertical and closer to horizontal; also known as slack angles

SKIPPING: a popping feeling in the drivetrain when you pedal hard; it occurs when a chain, cogset, and/or chainring is worn out

SPANNER: another word for wrench; applied to many bicycle tools

SPIDER: the multi-armed piece to which the chain wheels are bolted; usually part of the right crankarm

SPINDLE: a rod that rotates inside a body with a fixed orientation, such as a bottom bracket spindle or pedal spindle

SPOKE: one of several wires used to hold the hub in the center of a wheel rim and transfer the load from the perimeter of the wheel to the hub and onto the frame

SPORTS TOURER: a bicycle with structural strength, geometry, and components designed to make it a compromise between a bike suitable for racing and one suitable for loaded touring; good for general pleasure riding

SPROCKET: a disc bearing teeth for driving a chain; a general term that applies both to chainrings and to cassette cogs

STATIONARY TRAINER: a device to which you attach your bike so you can ride in place

STEEP ANGLES: angles that position frame tubes nearer to vertical than do shallow angles

STEERER TUBE: the tube that forms the top of the fork and rotates inside the head tube

STEM: the part that fits into (threaded) or onto (threadless) the fork's steerer tube and holds the handlebar

STRADDLE CABLE: a short cable on cantilever and centerpull-type brakes, each end of which attaches to a brake arm and is pulled up at the center to activate the brakes

STRADDLE HANGER: a triangular metal piece used to connect the main brake cable with the straddle cable of a centerpull or cantilever brake

STRAIGHT-GAUGE TUBING: see Plain-gauge tubing

SUSPENSION: a system of spring and damper that isolates a rider from the shock transmitted through the bike while riding over small obstacles such as rocks, roots, and potholes; a generic term referring to all types of sprung fork and frame designs

SWINGARM: the movable read end of a suspension bicycle

T

TANDEM: a bicycle that has seats, handlebars, and pedals for two or more riders, one behind the other

TAP: to cut threads inside a tube or opening; also the name of the tool that does the cutting

THREADED HEADSET: a type of headset that fits in to a fork with a threaded steerer tube; the threaded fitting is used to secure the fork and to adjust the headset bearing

THREADLESS HEADSET: a type of headset that fits on a fork with a threadless steerer tube; the headset parts and stem all fit to the outside of the fork steerer, and adjustment is made by compressing the assembly with a top cap before tightening the stem to secure everything

THREE-CROSS: a spoking pattern in which a spoke passes over two and under a third spoke before being attached to the rim

TOECLIPS AND TOE STRAPS: a cagelike kit attached to pedals to keep your feet in the correct position

TOP TUBE: the horizontal tube that connects the seat tube with the head tube

TRACK BIKE: a type of bike used for racing on a bicycle track; looks a lot like a road bike but features only one gear and has no brakes

TRIALS: a type of mountain bike competition that tests riders' abilities to negotiate large obstacles such as boulders, logs, and parked cars; these competitions are judged on technical ability rather than speed

TRIPLE CRANK: a triple-chainring crankset designed to provide a wide range of gears

TUBULAR: a type of tire that has a tube sewn inside the casing and is glued to the rim; also known as a sew-up

U

U-BRAKES: heavy-duty centerpull mountain bike brakes that affix to frame posts

UCI (UNION CYCLISTE INTERNATIONALE): the official international governing body for all disciplines of competitive cycling, including road, track, mountain bike, BMX, and cyclocross; recognized by the International Olympic Committee

ULTRA-MARATHON: a cross-country mountain bike race that covers a distance greater than 100 kilometers (62 miles)

UNICROWN FORK: a fork on which the blades curve in the top and are welded to the steerer to form the fork crown

UNIVERSAL CABLE: a shift or brake cable that's designed to fit all types of levers; on each end is a different lead end, and you cut off the one you don't need

USA CYCLING: the official governing body for all disciplines of competitive cycling in the United States, including road, track, mountain bike, BMX, and cyclocross; recognized by the United States Olympic Committee and the Union Cycliste Internationale

W

WHEELBASE: the distance between the front and rear axles

WIND TRAINER: a training device consisting of a frame in which a bicycle is fastened for stationary riding and a fan that creates wind resistance to simulate actual road riding

NOTES

PHOTO CREDITS